Rise TO THE Mission

Library of Congress Control Number: 2017949582

ISBN: 978-1-63308-278-6 (paperback)
       978-1-63308-279-3 (ebook)

Cover and Interior Design by *R'tor John D. Maghuyop*

CHALFANT ECKERT
PUBLISHING

1028 S Bishop Avenue, Dept. 178
Rolla, MO 65401

Printed in United States of America

Rise
TO THE
Mission

Believe It, Receive It, and Step Into It!

AMBER M. BROWN

CHALFANT ECKERT

PUBLISHING

THE UNSUNG HERO

I dedicate this book to my children, Aiden and Kyleigh. May you both rise above the difficulties of this world with grace and determination to complete your mission. In all you do, do it with love and respect. Things will come that will hurt you, try to stop you, and truly disappoint you, but even so, always remember that there is light at the end of tunnel. With God, all things are possible, and all things are made new in Him.

To my unsung hero,

You were my sunshine as a child, and now that I am older, I have come to truly respect and admire you not only for your courage and support but also for your heart and your spirit. You have always spoken the Word of God over my life, and I will be forever grateful. I know you are a background kind of man, but in my life, you have always been center stage. Thank you for always being there for us! I remember always singing to you as a little girl, and one day you said, "Baby, if you grow up to be a singer, promise me you will sing for the Lord." Well, God didn't bless me with vocals, but He did give me hands to write with, as well as words to honor Him. This book is for you Paw Paw!

Arise, shine, for your light has come, and the glory of the LORD has risen upon you.
Isaiah 60:1 ESV

FOREWORD

Amber Brown is a chosen vessel of God with a calling upon her life. She is a faithful servant of the Lord and a spiritual motivator that will awaken your soul and uplift your heart.

This book should be a required reading for every believer who has experienced major setbacks or perhaps you are at a standstill when you turn the pages of this book. As you read, this book will inspire you, encourage you, motivate you, and minister to you. Amber shares a piece of her life with us that will cause you to be challenged and will charge you to be awakened spiritually. It is time to answer the call and to Rise to your Mission that God has mandated for your life.

Dr. Ron Webb

Mt. Calvary Powerhouse Church,
Author of *Leadership Behind the Scenes,*
Destroying the Root of Racism, and
Exposing the Enemy from Behind the Scenes.

TABLE OF CONTENTS

ACKNOWLEDGMENTS

First and foremost, I would like to thank my Father in Heaven for making this book possible. Without you Lord, I would not be who I am today. You knew your vision for my life even before I was born, and because I chose to follow you, you made a way for me. Thank you for keeping your promises, and providing in me the strength needed to continue no matter what struggles I faced.

Secondly, I would like to thank my mom and dad for giving up the many things that you did so that my brother and I could have more. You shall never walk empty! Of all the sacrifices you have made, you will be given even more in return. I appreciate you two, and I am thankful for all you did, all you do, and all that you will continue to do in the future. Dad, the word *father* can mean a whole lot of things, but to me, it is your actions that make you a father. Thank you for rising to the mission, and being the man that we needed you to be; the father that we needed, but was missing for so long. I will always love you for that! Thank you, Nina and Papa, for always loving me through my good and my bad, for supporting me throughout the years, and for being there when my mother, brother, and I needed you the most. God sees what you do, and He repays you for the kind of people that you are. You are such wonderful grandparents, and I truly appreciate you both.

Last but certainly not least, I would like to thank my Pastor, Bishop Ron Webb, and First Lady Georgia Webb. You two have been wonderful and such an inspiration to my children and me. You have pushed me, pulled me, and encouraged me to be all that God has called me to be. I thank God for the both of you. He placed you in my life for a reason, and this season being one of them. Thank you, Bishop, for showing me that I could finish what I started. Thank you for being obedient and feeding my soul with the Word of God. God has used you to speak life into my dream that was held inside for far too long. Now, it is time to Rise to The Mission, and we are all doing it together!

...give, and it will be given to you.
Good measure, pressed down, shaken together,
running over, will be put into your lap. For with the
measure you use it will be measured back to you.
LUKE 6:38 ESV

INTRODUCTION

This book is for the believer and the unbeliever, a piece of encouragement to lift the heart of the unbeliever and to push the believer to do more! There is power within stillness, but there is also a movement of power that comes forth after being still for so long, and it causes you to rise! Change is always possible when you take the necessary steps to move forward. Whether you are a minister or an alcoholic that has turned your back on God, this book was written to inspire you and to show you that there is hope beyond your situation. We all have room to grow, and in the body of Christ, rising to the next level is a must. Just because you are a Christian doesn't mean that you won't ever have those moments in which you wonder what you are going to do. It comes with the territory. It may feel like you can't breathe now, but you will be able to take a deep breath and exhale after you give your situation over to God and trust Him to handle it. Trust God and make the move when you are ready, just as I had to. To rise means to move from a lower position to a higher one. We have all had moments of feeling that things could not get any worse, but it is in those moments when we are at our lowest that God is able to work best.

A mission is an important assignment. It is a piece to the pie that completes your story. How will your story end? Are you tired of not moving forward? Are you done asking why? Are you ready to get motivated and finish what you started? The things of this world have a way of distracting us, but it's time to get back on track. Have you fallen out of love with Jesus Christ? Do you blame God for the actions of others? Do you want to get close to Him, but don't know how? Do you question whether God is even real? We all need answers, and we all need to be resurrected in some area of our lives. I don't care who you are, what you do, how much money you have or pretend to have, we all need Jesus! This world has dried up. We need to come alive again. It is time for you to RISE, to get up out of that rut that you are in, and start living again. You have an amazing life full of possibilities waiting for you. Every morning you wake up is a second chance, and that means that God is not finished with you. All good things come from above so don't take anything for granted. Life is too short, so if you want change, you must first be the change!

God changed me and not just overnight, but over the years. He took the things that were hurting me and stunting my growth and replaced them with things that would restore me, cleanse me, and save my soul. I chose to listen to His voice and to humble myself, and for that, He has blessed me beyond measure.

Your life does not have to stay the same. The beauty of it all is that God didn't raise you up to just be a dead soul in this world. He has given you purpose and filled you with love and passion to complete your mission. You may or may not have experienced your passion yet, or you may not even know your purpose, but I pray that after reading this book that you will be closer to finding the rewritten you in Christ Jesus!

God has a plan for you, and it's to help make a difference in this world. He has raised you up for such a time as this, and I pray that this book surfaces the same passion in you that it has in me! Now is the time to walk in an unmovable faith and Rise to the Mission!

Do all things without grumbling or disputing, that you may be blameless and innocent, children of God without blemish in the midst of a crooked and twisted generation, among whom you shine as lights in the world, holding fast to the word of life, so that in the day of Christ I may be proud that I did not run in vain or labor in vain.
PHILIPPIANS 2:14-16 ESV

CHAPTER 1

Casted Out by Man,
but Chosen by God

But you are a chosen race, a royal priesthood,
a holy nation, a people for his own possession, that you
may proclaim the excellencies of him who called you out of
darkness into his marvelous light.
1 PETER 2:9 ESV

As a child, I always knew that I wanted to help change the world. I have come to realize that to change the world, I had to first change myself. I remember looking up at the stars and feeling a sense of comfort. It was like they pulled me in. I would grab my pillow and blanket, lie down on the trampoline, and start searching for answers. It was a place I could be myself and enjoy the beauty from above. I have always been a person to find the beauty in what most people ignore. I would ask myself why the stars shined so brightly every time I spend time with them. I believe that when you have the heart of a dreamer, the stars represent your passion. Each star carries something different that you will do in this life, and when you have completed that part of your mission, then another star gets in line to shine.

Lift up your eyes on high and see: who created these?
He who brings out their host by number, calling them all
by name; by the greatness of his might and because he is
strong in power, not one is missing.
ISAIAH 40:26 ESV

I think of us like God thinks of His stars. Every single one of us is here for a reason. We all have purpose and not one of us is in the wrong place. God knows why He created us. We may not understand, but it is not for us to understand. We are not worthy of His love, but because God had a vision, He gave each one of us a mission.

Man may cast you out, and you may feel that you are not capable of doing what God has called you to do because of others saying that you can't, but God never gives you purpose without equipping you for the mission. He is not a God that will allow you to fall on your face. He may allow you to trip so that you can learn from your mistakes, but He will just as quickly pick those feet up and tell you to keep on walking.

God is our refuge and strength,
a very present help in trouble.
PSALM 46:1 ESV

Jesus was casted out too. I use *casted* instead of *cast* because it is a word that was used for hundreds of years until modern times, and just sounds regal, more befitting of our Savior, King Jesus. God didn't say that the life here would be easy, but now that we can have a relationship with Jesus Christ, our life can be easier and less complicated. Jesus is the son of God who died on the cross and was a ransom for our sins. His blood was shed to form a blood covenant with God, a relationship that wouldn't be possible without the precious blood and love of Jesus Christ. God sent Him to this earth on a mission to save the world! Jesus came to save us from our sins so that we can have eternal life after death and so that our time here could be filled with love and reason. This world is our preparation zone, and it is time to start using the time that we have left to be focused and driven in the things of God, no matter what others say. We are running out of time brothers and sisters.

What would have happened if Jesus would have given up like we typically do? What would have happened if Jesus had given into His flesh and did not listen to Spirit of God? We wouldn't be able to have a relationship with Him; we would be stuck in our flesh and our wicked ways with no way out. This life would be followed by hell instead of heaven.

Why allow other people to influence your life? I know it hurts and it is hard not to get discouraged, but if we do as Jesus did and look to the Father and His Word, it will help every time. God chose you, and there is no one on earth who can take away the plans that God has for you, except YOU! That's right! You are your own worst enemy, and when you allow others to dictate your life, you make it easy for the devil to attack your heart, your mind, and your soul.

As you come to him, a living stone rejected by men but in the sight of God chosen and precious,
I Peter 2:4 ESV

There is power in the Word of God. None of us are perfect, and we will never be perfect, but the difference in a believer and a non-believer are that a non-believer does not believe in Jesus Christ and chooses to live a life that he or she wants in their own eyes and for their own reasons. A believer, on the other hand, is a child of God and is born again by faith in Jesus Christ. A believer will submit to God whom is unseen but is alive and active in his or her life, admit to not wanting to continue living the life that he or she is currently living, want to change, and want to follow the commandments of the Lord that have been written and set in stone for protection and guidance.

But he said to me, "My grace is sufficient for you, for my power is made perfect in weakness." Therefore I will boast all the more gladly of my weaknesses, so that the power of Christ may rest upon me. [10] For the sake of Christ, then, I am content with weaknesses, insults, hardships, persecutions, and calamities. For when I am weak, then I am strong.
II Corinthians 12:9-10 ESV

When God calls, you answer! Some may try to hold you back, others may tell you that you can't do it, but what do they really they know? Do they know the plans for your life? Are they people who should be giving you advice? Are they doing things and saying things to encourage you or to hold you back? These are tough questions, but God wants you to get rid of the people in your life that hold you back or make it difficult for you to move forward and get help. You cannot change without leaving your environment. If you truly want and need a change and want to start making a difference in your life and finding out who you truly are, then surround yourself with people who encourage you to be more. Find those people who love you enough to say, "Hey, you have to stop doing what you are doing," or "Hey, you can do anything you put your mind to."

You will need to let go of the things you currently love for the things that you can't live without later. In the future, you will realize how unimportant the things are that you think you need now. When that occurs, it's an amazing revelation. In the years, months, or even days to come, you may think back and realize how much God changed you and how He was your present help in your time of trouble. It is your faithfulness and obedience that brings forth God's promises. His timing is always the right timing, Amen! It is time to revise your soul and open your eyes, so you can unleash the power from within!

Open my eyes so that I may contemplate wonderful things from Your instruction.
PSALM 119:18 HOLMAN CHRISTIAN STANDARD BIBLE

Today is the day you say goodbye to those that have casted you out in the sea to drown and never return. Time to walk away from those who would rather see you fall then see you RISE and walk ahead of them. From this moment on, you will RISE above what has brought you down, and believe that you are needed, wanted, and meant for greatness no matter what other people say. Then you will walk each day with courage. There are many others out there who are just like I was and just like you are. We are held back by others, but God changes us little by little until we get to our points of arrival at our destinies, with passion in our hearts to continue and to never turn back.

The Position of Passion

John the Baptist had a mission, and it was to prepare the way for someone far greater than he, Jesus Christ! Within John's message, he was called to a baptism of repentance and the forgiveness of sins.

> *Every valley shall be exalted, and every mountain and hill*
> *shall be made low: and the crooked shall be made straight,*
> *and the rough places plain: And the glory of the LORD*
> *shall be revealed, and all flesh shall see it together:*
> *for the mouth of the LORD hath spoken it.*
> ISAIAH 40:4-5 KJV

John was in a position of passion which brought many to know Jesus for who He was and what He stood for. Let's think about the passion that hung on the cross. Jesus bled to His death, but gave us His life! The passion of Jesus Christ is the kind of passion that we should have.

All my life I have been a passionate person, but now that I follow God, my passion is stronger than ever. My passion now is to live for God and show people that Jesus loves them and is ready to come forth in their lives for the better. I must live a life in testimony and honor to Him because He saved me, changed me, blessed me, and continues to change and bless me. My passion and direction have changed but they are more fulfilling now that I know my purpose and what He has called me to do. You must look deep within and come to terms with other people not liking you or not believing in you. Not many will, but you will always be thankful for the certain few that God sends, and expect them to exactly what you need on your journey. You don't need multitudes of friends to be successful. You just need a few friends that will stand beside you and encourage you throughout the process.

Jesus didn't have many followers, but the ones He did have were specifically chosen. So, remember, you don't always get to choose who helps you and who hurts you, but if you leave it in God's hands, then you can rest assured that He will never allow you to go through anything that will not benefit you down the road. He always has a plan, and His plans are always to prosper you in the end.

Blessed are those who hunger
and thirst for righteousness, for they will be filled.
MATTHEW 5:6 NIV

My journey has been tough, but most definitely worth it! God never designed us to stay the same. He made us unique, and He developed us to handle growth and maturity. You have been growing since you were in your mother's womb, and God knew you even then. He has always had big plans for you, which is why it is important for you to allow your passion to burn within you and allow Him to guide you down the path that brings light, salvation, and freedom.

Over the years, I have come to realize that it is much harder to live saved than it is to live in sin. What a difference, but I wouldn't go back to my old life, not for one second. I still have some rough days (and you will too), but now my life has changed. Now that I put my faith in God and not people, I live differently, think differently, act differently, and love differently. I now understand that once I gave my life to Jesus Christ, I gained salvation, put my faith into action, and my life started getting better even though I was still going through hard times.

Count it all joy, my brothers, when you meet trials of various
kinds, for you know that the testing of your faith produces
steadfastness. And let steadfastness have its full effect,
that you may be perfect and complete, lacking in nothing.
JAMES 1:2-4 ESV

God provides us with much more than man could ever give us. If you don't know all the things that God has for you, then I encourage you to get out your Bible. Yes, the one that is on the shelf collecting dust, and get your passion back. There is victory in Jesus Christ. In Him, you have already won the battle!

But thanks be to God, which giveth us the victory
through our Lord Jesus Christ.
I CORINTHIANS 15:57 KJV

When giving up the reigns of control in your life, it is like a tide coming in, but it will be the best wave you have ever seen. You have the chance to either make it through this life with happiness and everlasting life, or you can choose to join the others who have fallen and lost their passion and drive, never to return, those who will never see the pearly gates or taste the sweetness of eternal life.

Blessed is the man that endureth temptation: for when he is tried, he shall receive the crown of life, which the Lord hath promised to them that love him.
James 1:12 KJV

But we are not of them who draw back unto perdition; but of them that believe to the saving of the soul.
Hebrews 10:39 KJV

The only way that the enemy can win is if you remain silent. Jesus died and rose so that even though you die, you may also rise. Without Him, you may not be able to face the things of this world and overcome them. Without Jesus, we would be living in fear and condemnation for the rest of our lives. We would be the outcasts until death and the laughter in the heart of the enemy. But Jesus was chosen to build a bridge between you and God. Now, you can rise just as Jesus did and believe in your heart that God has chosen you for such a time as this. His strength is within us, and if we look deep down within our souls, we will find Him: His face, His voice, His love, and His Word. When you find Him, hold Him close, and don't allow anyone to cause you to ever let Him go. You can overcome anything with the right mindset and with great passion. It is time to believe that you are a child of the living God. If you don't already know, receive His Word and His vision for your life, and step into your destiny! For those who casted you out, God says "Denied!" You're accepted and enrolled in *The University of Salvation and Acceptance,* not the *University of Adversity and Condemnation.*

CHAPTER 2

Salvation is the Number One Formation

Now faith is the substance of things hoped for,
the evidence of things not seen.
HEBREWS 11:1 KJV

O ne of the key ingredients to being prosperous and finding your passion is first walking in formation within your salvation, the kind of formation that blesses you from the crown of your head to the souls of your feet. I didn't know God then like I know Him now, it has been a process. If you are a beginner, don't get discouraged. It takes time, but I have grown to love and trust Him. I have a deep respect for who He is and what He stands for. I am thankful that as a young child, among all the pain I was experiencing, I had someone who knew how good God was, and filled my mind with His love. God will choose people to be there when you need them, and thankfully this person was my great grandfather.

You make known to me the path of life;
in your presence there is fullness of joy; at your right hand
are pleasures forevermore.
PSALM 16:11 ESV

When I was younger, my great grandparents read the Word of God to me in their living room after dinner. I remember to this day the happiness in their hearts to be able to share that part of their lives with my brother and me. I didn't always want to sit there and listen because sometimes I was sent to their house after I had gotten into trouble, but my mother knew just what to do. After a shower, I laid down for bed, and my great grandparents would both put their hands on my head and pray for me. The power that I felt was unexplainable when they put their hands on my head and started praying to God. Now I understand, but then I had no idea what they were doing and why they were doing it. It is important for us as parents, grandparents, siblings, and other relatives to pray for those we love. That played a huge part in my salvation. Never fear praying for others, if they allow you to, and know that God is the one giving the power and because of Him, their hearts will be touched in some way. What you do for the Lord is never in vain.

Therefore, my dear brothers and sisters, be steadfast, immovable, always excelling in the Lord's work, because you know that your labor in the Lord is not in vain.
I CORINTHIANS 15:58 CSB

Salvation is what led me here and caused me to write this book. I did not know when God's Word over my life would come to pass, but I am so thankful that because of my salvation, and because He has restored me, that I was able to write this book for all of you. God uses us differently, but when we accomplish parts of our mission, we bless others. Never think that something is not for you. Never assume anything is unreachable. NO matter who you were, or what kind of conditions you grew up in, if God says it is for you, "Then Baby, it's for you!"

Salvation means the preservation or deliverance from harm, ruin, or loss (*English Oxford Living Dictionary*, 2017). It is your lifeline, your redemption, and your deliverance. When we are stuck in our flesh, we really don't think about these things, and the last thing we want to do is change. We tell ourselves repeatedly that we are just fine right where we are. Well, the devil is a liar! (John 8:44). That is the most untrue thing that the enemy will try to put into our minds. Who really wants to stay the same and never grow and mature? Who really wants to keep doing drugs and living daily in sadness and shame? Nobody! The enemy attacks our minds with lies and stunts our progress by planting untrue thoughts of our inability to change. We must be very careful what we listen to and who we walk beside because our lives depend on it!

for all have sinned and fall short of the glory of God,
ROMANS 3:23 ESV

Gordon Allport (1937) once said, "The outstanding characteristic of man is individuality ... There was never a person just like you, and there never will be again." It is the same for God. There will never be anyone like God nor will others do the things for you that God has done for you.

In this the love of God was made manifest among us,
that God sent his only Son into the world,
so that we might live through him.
I JOHN 4:9 ESV

God saw that we had drifted far away from Him, and for His vision to manifest, He sent Jesus Christ to die for us so that He could be risen. God loves you despite the good and the bad; His love for you never fades. He may get angry with you from time to time, and you may disappoint Him more often than you would like, but even though you (or I) are not worthy of His love and His grace, He gives it to you anyway. To have salvation in Jesus Christ, we must first acknowledge Him as our Lord, ask for His forgiveness, believe that God raised Him from the dead, and be ready to live for Him.

If you declare with your mouth, "Jesus is Lord,"
and believe in your heart that God raised him from the
dead, you will be saved. For it is with your heart that you
believe and are justified, and it is with your mouth that
you profess your faith and are saved.
ROMANS 10:9-10 NIV

When I first gave my life to God, I was scared. I was just a little girl who didn't feel that I was worthy of love. I was hurt, unable to trust, and lonely inside. My biological father was sexually abusing me. While growing up, I saw physical abuse in homes, including my own, and I dealt with mental and emotion abuse as well. The very people who I was supposed to be able to trust were the ones who were hurting me. How do you speak up when no one is there to listen? Many of us have this issue and still hurt today. However, the moment I broke was the moment I felt God's presence and love for the very first time.

I remember the difference in how I felt depending on the church I went to. I once was invited to a church that only hurt me and left me walking out the door with frustration and questions. They told me that little girls should wear dresses and not wear pants, that I looked like a boy and should wear a dress next time. That stayed with me for a long time, and I remember thinking, "Wow, is this how people are supposed to be treated?" and "Is this what God is really about?" The sadness in it all is that people still act like that with newcomers in the church and it drives away. It is important to be careful how you treat others because you could be the cause of their fall.

I was a tomboy growing up that would rather wear a t-shirt and jeans than a dress. It wasn't until these last five years that God has really brought out the beautiful woman in me that loves myself for who I am. I still love my jeans, I still love fishing and getting dirty, and I am not scared to pull over and change my own tire, but God has really developed in me a mighty Christian woman who has finally found ME, but only because I allowed myself to be molded by Him.

For we are His creation,
created in Christ Jesus for good works, which God prepared
ahead of time so that we should walk in them.
EPHESIANS 2:10 HOLMAN CHRISTIAN STANDARD BIBLE

After I got over what had been done to me at that church, I decided to try an old Baptist church. I sat there and sang the church hymns as if I knew what they meant. I didn't know much about God at the time, but

I knew the things my grandfather had told me, and I knew that he had power in his hands when he had prayed for me. So, I opened my heart up that day to believe all that had been told to me. I needed a miracle. I needed something to believe in that was going to be true, and not be a lie like everything else in my life. That is how I felt walking in the doors of that church, which is probably why I received what I did. When we walk with expectancy and need, we tend to walk out with more than what we walked in with. I had to be willing to pay attention and listen. I had to allow my walls to fall so that His Word could replace my brokenness at that moment. I walked in as I was. I wasn't perfect; I didn't have everything under control. I was broken and messed up, but God still accepted me as I was. Many people feel that they must be perfect or clean up their acts before walking into the sanctuary. Praise God that is not the case! We would not have churches because none of us would be able to step foot into the door. Don't allow the enemy to convince you that you must have it all together before you go to church, he is a liar! Go as you are and God will be there to welcome you with open arms.

After the pastor preached and the piano music started playing, I felt a sudden pull on my heart. As I got down on my knees in this very small sanctuary, I placed my head on the bench, and my hands over my face, and I cried like a baby. I poured my heart out to God. I couldn't understand why such bad things were happening to me if He loved me. I knew that I was a good person, but I didn't understand why I was not living the life that I was meant to live. But how do we really know what life is planned for us? Truth is, we don't.

This poor man cried, and the LORD heard him And saved him out of all his troubles.
PSALM 34:6 NASB

After much crying, I came to a moment of silence. I could feel a sense of relief come over me, like there was nothing more to fear and that God was going to take care of me. I felt like He heard me and let me know that He was listening. Someone walked up to me and she started praying over me. I accepted Jesus Christ as my Lord and Savior, and that night I was saved! God can touch you and save you at any age if you just make room for Him.

The woman that prayed with me cared for me and was sent from God to bring me to salvation. That is how we should make others feel. We should not force them to believe how we believe, but just be there for them. Share what God has done for you, and find out what their needs are. I felt love and compassion from her. She cared about my salvation, just as I care about your salvation. I love helping others, and I love how God uses me to help others, but the real MVP is God. In God's eyes, your soul is worth saving. He values you and wants a relationship with you now and in eternity.

At the very moment God saved me, I started believing in Him even though I couldn't trust anyone in the world. Jesus was now my answer. He was the component needed to save my life. I felt more peace after accepting Jesus Christ than I ever felt before. Even though I was a little girl, I moved from death to life as soon as I chose to let go of everything that I had been carrying, and gave it all to Him. My tears and conversation with Him were the very things I needed to break that yoke of bondage and sadness in my life so that I could move forward.

Cast your cares on the LORD and he will sustain you;
he will never let the righteous be shaken.
PSALM 55:22 NIV

Start the Formation

There is a hidden masterpiece in you just waiting to be seen. Some of you have already been saved, some of you don't even know if you're ready to take that step, and some are thinking that now is the time to say, "YES!" to God. If that is you, God is ready to start this journey with you. He has always been ready; He has just been waiting on you. If you are ready to walk this out with God at your side, then you must first be saved and accept Jesus Christ as your Lord and Savior and repent of your sins. The first order of obedience after accepting Christ is to be baptized in water. God has many gifts for His family (of which you are part once you accept Christ), and one of those gifts is to receive the Holy Spirit. When Jesus ascended to Heaven, he sent the Holy Spirit to be a comforter and teacher for you. Once saved, you are indwelled by the Holy Spirit, which means that God's Spirit lives inside of you, guiding you and leading you in righteousness. The Holy Spirit brings many fruits to you and they are a package deal, one inseparable fruit of love, joy, peace, patience, kindness, goodness, faithfulness, gentleness and self-control (Galatians 5:22). You can also be baptized in the Holy Spirit and speak in tongues.

Repent, then, and turn to God,
so that your sins may be wiped out, that times
of refreshing may come from the Lord,
ACTS 3:19 NIV

Then Peter said unto them, Repent and be baptized each
one of you into the name of Jesus Christ for the remission
of sins, and ye shall receive the gift of the Holy Spirit.
ACTS 2:38 JUBILEE BIBLE 2000

If you have already asked Jesus Christ to be your Lord and Savior, I ask you to pray for those who have not. There are many out there; you may even be one of them reading this book right now. If you are feeling a little tug on your heartstrings, then God is speaking to you. For those who are lost but want to be found, here are a couple of Scriptures to look over, read, and meditate on until you are ready to take the leap of faith. There are prayers throughout the Bible that you can turn to for help, especially in Psalms. The plan of salvation is a process, but I promise you that God will see you through just as He has done for me.

Thou hast thrust sore at me that I might fall: but the
Lord helped me. The Lord is my strength and song, and is
become my salvation. The voice of rejoicing and salvation
is in the tabernacles of the righteous: the right hand of the

*Lord doeth valiantly. The right hand of the Lord is exalted:
the right hand of the Lord doeth valiantly. I shall not die,
but live, and declare the works of the Lord. The Lord hath
chastened me sore: but he hath not given me over unto
death. Open to me the gates of righteousness: I will go into
them, and I will praise the Lord: This gate of the Lord, into
which the righteous shall enter. I will praise thee: for thou
hast heard me, and art become my salvation.*
PSALM 118:13-21 KJV

*He that dwelleth in the secret place of the most High shall
abide under the shadow of the Almighty. I will say of the
Lord, He is my refuge and my fortress: my God; in him
will I trust. Surely he shall deliver thee from the snare
of the fowler, and from the noisome pestilence. He shall
cover thee with his feathers, and under his wings shalt
thou trust: his truth shall be thy shield and buckler. Thou
shalt not be afraid for the terror by night; nor for the arrow
that flieth by day; Nor for the pestilence that walketh in
darkness; nor for the destruction that wasteth at noonday.
A thousand shall fall at thy side, and ten thousand at thy
right hand; but it shall not come nigh thee. Only with
thine eyes shalt thou behold and see the reward of the
wicked. Because thou hast made the Lord, which is my
refuge, even the most High, thy habitation;*
PSALM 91:1-9 KJV

Most people don't want to admit that they have a problem or are living unjustly, but it is amazing how blind we really are until God gives us a new pair of glasses and a new way of thinking.

*But God hath revealed them unto us by his Spirit: for the
Spirit searcheth all things, yea, the deep things of God.*
I CORINTHIANS 2:10 KJV

As believers, we cannot truly see and understand God if we are not trying to live for Him. For unbelievers, they cannot truly know themselves until they know who they are in Christ. We must seek Him, search out His Word, search Him in prayer, and allow the Holy Spirit to reveal Himself to us. We experience these things and gain understanding through salvation, which is why it is so important. The enemy brings much confusion and disorder into this world, but Jesus died for you and rose three days later so that you could rise above the plots and plans of the enemy as well. We are here to be witnesses of the power of God. If God can raise the dead, He can raise the sinner! The moment that God raised Jesus from the grave was the very moment that He showed His power over life and death. Rise to The Mission, brothers and sisters, and start your formation process. Find your salvation in Christ! First step: Forgiveness.

Jesus saith unto him, I am the way, the truth, and the life: no man cometh unto the Father, but by me.
JOHN 14:6 KJV

CHAPTER 3

The Broken Wing of Unforgiveness

And whenever you stand praying, forgive, if you have anything against anyone, so that your Father also who is in heaven may forgive you your trespasses.
MARK 11:25 ESV

Be angry and do not sin; do not let the sun go down on your anger, and give no opportunity to the devil.
EPHESIANS 4:26-27 ESV

Your wings are an important part of your travels. When one of them is broken or bruised, it is hard to fly. Without both wings, you cannot be lifted, elevated, or moved as God has intended. Many of us find it hard to forgive others, but let me be real with you, God will not continue to forgive you if you can't find it in your heart to forgive others. Unfortunately, when you carry unforgiveness, you bruise your wings, which holds you back.

The LORD is a refuge for the oppressed, a stronghold in times of trouble.
PSALM 9:9 NIV

Unforgiveness is one of the most powerful bondages that the enemy can use to hold you captive. Yes, it hurts, Yes, it is hard to trust, but you learn to forgive the sinner and let God forgive the sin! Trust me, it is NOT easy, but you will gain power in your struggles if you forgive those who have caused you pain. The power of God is your warfare. Hard pill to swallow, I know, but we must deal with hurt each day from the actions and decisions of the world, as well as our self-afflicted actions and decisions. However, if we choose to have hearts like God and let go of that hurt, we will gain His power which sustains us through even our darkest hours! He sends people to help you get through each day.

Give justice to the weak and the fatherless; maintain the right of the afflicted and the destitute.
PSALM 82:3 ESV

If we keep regret, rejection, hatred, and jealousy in our hearts, we die. Our souls are dead! Our hearts are beating, but we are not fully living! What kind of life is that? Why would you want to hold a grudge with your brother or sister when God forgives you each day? You look down on your brother and sister for doing something, but you do the same thing. Don't turn into the very thing that you dislike. So many of us, and I have been guilty myself, say one thing but then turn around and do the very same thing we just told someone else not to do. It happens, but hypocrites are everywhere we go. Choose not to be one! God wants us to stand out, not stand with the crowd. We can't stand out when we act like everyone else. Right? That's right ... Fist Bump, then Blow it up!

Even with the daily struggles of this world, it is nice to know that with God, joy always comes in the morning. Without God, you may have happiness now, but without His protection and covering, unfortunately when the battles come, some of them you will have to fight on your own. God will still protect the unbeliever at the moments that are planned by God, but a believer's life is always in God's hands which is why we give our battles to Him to fight. It is difficult at the end of the day, when you're all upset and frustrated, to have a conversation with God. So, what do you do? You go to bed without giving God all your emotion and negative thinking from that day which then bottles up and causes you to explode later. Christians, I bet if we spoke to God every morning and every night before bed, we would probably have better days and finer nights.

The Bible says, "Joy comes in the morning" (Psalm 30:5) because when we give our daily struggles to God before laying down to rest, we wake up with new beginnings and a brand-new day. We are not holding on to those feelings because we already gave them away. How can we keep something that we already gave away, right? I understand that it hurts now, I know that it takes time to let go, but I also know that if we stay true to the Word of God and trust Him, then all will be well!

He heals the brokenhearted and binds up their wounds.
PSALM 147:3 NIV

There is freedom where the Spirit of the Lord is so when you lean on God, when you pray, when you ask the Holy Spirit to take over, it is at those times that God bring peace over your mind and comfort to your soul. Rise and become one who comes to terms with not having control over others or their actions, and allow God to use you no matter what else is going on in the world around you. You change yourself first so that you can help make a difference in this world! It all starts with you and me!

Get rid of all bitterness, rage and anger,
brawling and slander, along with every form of malice.
Be kind and compassionate to one another, forgiving each
other, just as in Christ God forgave you.
EPHESIANS 4:31-32 NIV

Hey, this season too shall pass! Instead of holding grudge, go to your brothers or sisters and work it out! It is your moment to break the chains of unforgiveness and move on with your life. It also allows them to move on with their lives as well. Don't be someone who holds someone else back because of the discontent in your own heart. Start forgiving, and you will start noticing your blessings multiply. God's promises are true, and when we follow His Word and guidance, He reveals confirmation, and He lets us know that we are doing right by Him.

Come to me, all who labor and are heavy laden,
and I will give you rest.
MATTHEW 11:28 ESV

God will give us a little bit of insight into His love and goodness within our spirit man, then in our outward man, just as a father or mother would. When you follow your parents' rules, you are rewarded. God is the same way! You live by the rules set forth by God, and He rewards you. When you are living in His house, you live by His rules.

The Story Untold

As a child, my life was not one that I would want to live again. I too had to learn to forgive to get to the place that I am at today spiritually and emotionally. I grew up in a home full of abuse, alcohol, and violence. I had to live with things that a child should not have to go through or see. I believe that the life that I lived has made me wise beyond my years, and God can now use me to help those who are going through similar circumstance or that have gone through them in the past.

I had to learn the hard way what not to do and who not to become. Alcoholism breaks down families and individuals in ways that make it hard to recover. An excessive drinker or alcoholic with anger and aggression issues can cause injury or death to himself or those around him. That was the case for me. I saw people I loved get abused, and I couldn't do anything about it. I didn't have a voice that was loud enough or tough enough to handle the consequences.

Before you know it, the actions of others start bleeding and attaching themselves to other members of the family and the same characteristics start developing and shaping you. This is what the enemy does. He uses earthly things like abuse and chemical dependency to give an excuse for people to hurt those they love. It forms a cycle for the next person in line until death overtakes them and sin is created. It is a game of control and manipulation by the enemy, and it is hard to find your way out. I haven't seen my biological father since I was a child. I do not know where he is, who he has turned out to be, or if he is dead or alive. Still yet, I have chosen to Rise above my past and to forgive him for the things he did to me. When you forgive someone, you truly want to make sure that they are okay as well. That is the God in you! Even though I dealt with horrible things, I really want to make sure that he is okay and to let him know that I am okay too, but I still haven't gotten the chance to. I trust God on this one though.

And we know that in all things God works
for the good of those who love him, who have been
called according to his purpose.
ROMANS 8:28-29 NIV

No child should ever have to feel unloved, but when you are not mature enough to understand or comprehend the things that are happening around you, that is how you are going to feel. As a believer, I understand that abusers allow the enemy to take over their minds causing them to commit wrongful acts. It was the spirit inside of my father that hurt me, not him! And I pray that he has given his life to Christ and has formed a new life and healthy relationships with others.

In my prayer time, I often thank God for all of the people I have helped because of my experiences with my father, and the ones who I will help in the future because of my past. There were times I thought about suicide, but I am thankful that I had people around me who helped me through it. I look back now and am grateful I did not believe the lies of the enemy. How many people will fall if you are not there to be a witness to them? I chose not to continue to live in my past hurts and failures! I chose to RISE and be the exception! Now it is time for you to be the exception. There are many people, especially teenagers, who think about killing themselves and some actually follow through with it. Suicide is such a tragic event and is happening more often than we might realize. We all need to come together to do all that we can to prevent this from taking the lives of those we love and care about. It starts with you reaching out and helping those that are showing signs of wanting to commit suicide. Depression, bipolar disorder, personality disorders, schizophrenia, and anxiety are just some of the signs. You never know what someone is capable of until it is too late. So please Rise to The Mission and be a voice for those who cannot speak up for themselves in times of despair.

Every day matters and not only for you but others too. Someone is counting on you just as you are counting on them. It's funny because what the enemy meant for evil in my life, God turned into good, just as He will your life! He had a plan for me just as He does for you and the ones who you know are hurting. I had no idea that all that pain I went through was going to be a powerful testimony today.

There was a void in my life after I moved out of my parents' house and lived on my own. I was ready to grow up, but I wasn't ready for the consequences to come. I eventually made a wrong turn. It is easy to get caught up in the things of the world when you have less protection around you, so I always encourage young adults and youth to stay with their parents until they are ready to move out mentally, physically, and financially. I didn't have family or friends around to tell me not to sin or to pick me up when I fell. All I had was myself, and there came a time when I allowed other people to speak the wrong things in my ear which led me to self-destruction. Thank God it was only for a season. I had to heal from some decisions that I had made just as you must take time to heal. Don't allow others to make you feel bad about decisions that you have made because we must learn to make our own decisions and learn from them. We must also accept the consequences and repercussions that result from those decisions. Understand that you are important and you must break through whatever it is that is trying to break you. Know when to bounce back. I know that even though I wasn't going to God at the time, He was still coming to me. I might have got off route, but God never gets lost. You might be found in exile, but remember, you were birthed for promise!

*because human anger does not produce
the righteousness that God desires.*
JAMES 1:20 NIV

When people are angry within themselves and do not ask for God's healing over their lives, their anger and lashing out gets misdirected to others, sometimes resulting in physical or sexual abuse. God does not want us to act out in these ways or be put in these situation by others, so He provides us with Scripture so that if we ever feel the need to sin, we can go to His Word and get healing.

In James 1:20, we learn that anger does not produce the righteousness that God desires. Anger is bottled up inside many people. How do you think it makes others feel to have to live with your sadness and pain because you can't let things go? What are you doing to others that you shouldn't be doing because of your own resistance? What if I told you that all that bottled-up anger and emotion can be taken away without abusing and hurting other people?!?! There is help out there for those that need it, but first, you must get rid of the pride and face your problems. I implore those of you who choose to abuse other people because of your anger: Please get help before you touch another person or speak death into someone's life! I dealt with abuse as a child and while growing up and I wouldn't want that for you or anyone. Abuse, whether dishing it out or being the recipient, gives the devil an opening inside our heads. He uses things like this to make people bitter, angry, and untrusting, just to keep this evil cycle going. Choose not to be the person consumed and controlled by anger. Ask God to help you overcome these emotions and start finding Scriptures that correlate with your issues. You may not be having issues with this personally, but if you know someone who is the abused or is the abuser, please share this book with them and help them find resources in the community to save their lives.

When I was younger, I couldn't make everything okay, but I felt like I could. I felt like the hero of my own story but had no one to play the other roles needed to have a happy ending. You can never accomplish anything on your own. There will always be someone who helped guide you along the way. Help others get through their anger. Be an active positive influence in your community so that the next generation is stronger and happier with less hurt and anger.

Through the praise of children and infants you have
established a stronghold against your enemies, to silence
the foe and the avenger.
PSALM 8:2 NIV

Start children off on the way they should go, and even
when they are old they will not turn from it.
PROVERBS 22:6 NIV

There is power in the word **NO.** I often think of people who can't find the strength to turn away from the grip of the enemy. With each passing day, there is something new that the enemy puts on this earth for God's people to turn to in an effort to solve all their problems. If it is from the devil, you may think that it solves all your problems momentarily, but the consequences will last you a lifetime.

My God sent His angel and shut the lions' mouths and
they have not harmed me, inasmuch as I was found
innocent before Him; and also toward you, O king,
I have committed no crime
DANIEL 6:22 NASB

Take charge of your situation because even though you may be addicted now, whatever the addiction may be, you must say, "NO!"

You must RISE TO THE MISSION, and save your life from destruction just as I did. You deserve more, but it is up to you to take a step of faith and GO!

You know, it is hard for others to RISE in situations without help or support. So, if you are someone who needs help, but doesn't feel like you have anyone, then take me writing this book as motivation for you to get up and to get you walking down the path that God intended for you to walk. Call your nearest health clinic or hospital. They will get you to the appropriate resources that will help you along the way. Let go of that pride and ask for help. There is nothing wrong with asking for help. I understand that most people will hold things against you, and throw things in your face, but you never know who God will use in your life to help you if you will just break your walls down and ask them for help. Many people are broken and carry so much hurt, but can I be honest with you? You will get hurt throughout life, but that doesn't mean you have to continue living the life that you are living. You chose your life; it didn't choose you, which means that any given time you can choose a different life. I learned that making better choices brought me better results. There comes a time when you must decide that you are going to live and not die, even if it means giving up others and all that you carry with you that belongs to them. You allowed them to become a part of you, and it's time to let them go.

Sometimes God will allow something extreme to happen to get people to move. Maybe you have lost your job, your home, your children, your friends or family; there comes a time when God stops waiting on you and makes decisions for you. You may feel as if you are alone in these situations, but God is always with you. Ask Him for help!

Forgive But Never Forget

Because of the life I had lived and things I have watched others go through, I developed much empathy and compassion for people who go through emotional, physical, and sexual abuse. You may seem like the victim during the situation, but when you give all that hurt and pain to God when you seek His truth, you will find the freedom that you need to get past it. It may seem like a bad thing now, but God is going to take your turmoil and struggles and add them to your testimony!

> *But as for you, ye thought evil against me;*
> *but God meant it unto good, to bring to pass,*
> *as it is this day, to save much people alive.*
> GENESIS 50:20 KJV

Sometimes we must go through tough and challenging times, but God doesn't like us going through them. He cries for us just as I cried for my mother. He weeps tears of sadness and compassion when things happen, but it is our job to find Him in the moments when tears drip from our cheeks. Our sadness is no surprise to God, we do not catch Him off guard or unable to respond to our need.

How can you help others if you haven't gone through things like death, addiction, suffering, betrayal, and the sinfulness of this world? How is God supposed to reach the people going through these situations if He doesn't have witnesses here on earth? Be the witness that He needs you to be. You did not go through what you did just to continue hurting; He is calling you to RISE and use that pain for others' benefit. When I was struggling, I did not know His plan for my life, but now that I do, I don't want to ever quit on Him. I want to keep growing and moving forward. We must elevate our relationship with Him and always remain teachable and willing to forgive those who hurt us or spitefully use or abused us.

> *Likewise, you who are younger,*
> *be subject to the elders. Clothe yourselves,*
> *all of you, with humility toward one another, for*
> *"God opposes the proud but gives grace to the humble."*
> I PETER 5:5 ESV

When you present yourself with a humble heart and truly want forgiveness, God will help you pick yourself back up again and start where you left off, and He expects you to give the same courtesy to your brother, sister, mother, or father, both in your biological family and in your spiritual family.

> *Then Peter came to Jesus and asked, "Lord, how many*
> *times shall I forgive my brother or sister who sins against*
> *me? Up to seven times?" Jesus answered, "I tell you, not*
> *seven times, but seventy-seven times.*
> MATTHEW 18:21-22 NIV

Say it with me, "No more playing the victim!"

Lift your head up, open up those beautiful eyes and say, "God, please forgive me for not forgiving others. I thank you for turning my pain into compassion and my hurt into love! I will no longer be ashamed or unforgiving of what happened in the past, but I now understand that you are turning all of this pain into happiness for my future."

Keep in mind that wanting brings planning; planning produces action; with action comes results; results make progress, and progress brings achievement. Thank God for the people in your life who are helping you to become a better person, and thank God for the people who left. There is a lesson in everything. In many lessons, there is a wrongdoing but a positive outcome. It is time to live in the now, let go of your past, forgive others, and allow God to take care of your future.

Sometimes we need the gravel to slow us down so that we can appreciate the smoothness of the highway. The road less traveled tends to be the roughest because not many have had to conquer it, but the greatness of those who have made it to the end is that they live to tell it!

Thou hast beset me behind and before,
and laid thine hand upon me.
PSALM 139:5 KJV

Don't settle for the bad, but go through it so that you can learn to appreciate the good. Both are very special parts of your growth and your walk with God. I have learned to let go and move on, but it took me a while to overcome the fear and rejection held me hostage for many years. If you feel this way, you are not alone. I could not be set free from what happened until I asked God to heal me. The light in this comes from God. From my experiences as a child and young adult, I learned to recognize the signs of abuse in men and women. I can sense abusers' spirits, which makes it easier to pray for others and to help them. God will give you the same discernment, but you must first surrender.

After your surrender, God will heal your mind and your soul and will put you back together little by little until you finally become free from your past and your present sufferings. There are still bumps in the road ahead, but when you acknowledge and feed the need with God's nourishment, then you can live a more stable lifestyle with a sound mind. When you leave an unstable and unhealthy environment, your life changes. You think and react differently.

For all the parents out there: Parents, if you don't grow up, your children won't grow up either. Look inside the looking glass and let go of that wounded inner child.

And after you have suffered a little while,
the God of all grace, who has called you to his eternal glory
in Christ, will himself restore, confirm, strengthen,
and establish you.
I Peter 5:10 ESV

CHAPTER 4

The Wounded Inner Child: Inside the Looking Glass

The Lord is near to the brokenhearted
and saves the crushed in spirit.
PSALM 34:18 ESV

"I have often reflected that the causes of success or failure of men depend upon their character and nature, and (are) not a matter of choice," said Niccolo Machiavelli (*The Prince*, p. 33, 2017). When I think about this, I believe that in my heart it is true. The only thing I would want to add is that we first cannot control our failures or successes as children. Sometimes things are put on us without our doing; sometimes we follow the wrong people because we are told to, or we are raised in an environment which hurts us and causes failure in us before we are even old enough to recognize the cause.

We all have a spiritual journey. With everything there is a beginning and an end; especially when it comes to our stages of life. God starts with Genesis and ends with Revelation. Our training ground begins after we learn how to understand and develop our own ways of thinking. It is then that we form opinions of how we should be, what we should think, or whether our feelings are accurate or not, in the eyes of others and ourselves. Your inner child is formed at infancy, but when you become abused and hurt, that wounded inner child needs to leave so that you can be made stronger, wiser, and become more capable of being a leader and not a follower of the wrong people.

When I was a child, I used to speak like a child, think like a child, reason like a child; when I became a man, I did away with childish things.
I CORINTHIANS 13:11 NASB

Now is the time to start growing and developing in your relationship with Jesus Christ and with yourself, and leave that wounded inner child behind. No more talking about it, but make the decision right now to start doing something about it! Form a game plan, work out a strategy, and get the ball rolling! If you can't let go of your wounded inner child, you will never become all that God has created you to be. You will dream it, you will crave it, you will want it day in and day out, but if you are not doing what is necessary to grow and push yourself past your comfort zone, then you will never be able to handle the higher-level callings. Listen up! You will find contentment within yourself at the very moment you realize that you are done wondering about what other people are doing, and you start focusing on the work YOU must do!

Look carefully then how you walk, not as unwise but as wise, making the best use of the time, because the days are evil. Therefore do not be foolish, but understand what the will of the Lord is.
EPHESIANS 5:15-17 ESV

What has God called you to do? We have much work to do brothers and sisters! We don't have time to be playing games with the enemy. With every hardship comes opportunity. So, see this as an opportunity to set yourself apart from the rest. Let go of the wounded inner child holding you back, and start taking faith steps into your destiny!

"It is through healing our inner child, our inner children, by grieving the wounds that we suffered, that we can change our behavior patterns and clear our emotional process. We can release the grief with its pent-up rage, shame, terror, and pain from those feeling places which exist within us"

ROBERT BURNEY

Codependence: The Dance of Wounded Souls, A Cosmic Perspective of Codependence and the Human Condition (2012).

Many of the people you will meet can easily change for others, but there will be those few diamonds in the rough who will stay true to who they really are! A person's mentality needs to be at a certain level to make a positive difference in the world. Holding your wounded inner child hostage in your heart and mind is only going to bring pain and unneeded suffering in the long run. We cannot help others if we are not willing to help ourselves. We don't want to lead others in the wrong direction, so if we are operating under an immature mindset or under childlike authority, then we will pass that on to others, limiting their development and individuality. That is one reason we have the problems we have in our generation. The morals and ethics taught to the younger generation are not appropriate and are holding us back from growing into strong leaders of America. But, we can Rise to The Mission and change this; there is always hope!

Praise be to the God and Father of our Lord Jesus Christ! In his great mercy he has given us new birth into a living hope through the resurrection of Jesus Christ from the dead, and into an inheritance that can never perish, spoil or fade. This inheritance is kept in heaven for you, who through faith are shielded by God's power until the coming of the salvation that is ready to be revealed in the last time. In all this you greatly rejoice, though now for a little while you may have had to suffer grief in all kinds of trials.

I PETER 1:3-6 NIV

Change occurs every minute of every day. I always say that if we are changing, make sure we are changing for the Lord. In this case, if we are changing for the better then change is going to cause a positive impact on our lives and the lives of others! You are not going to be ready to do some things, and that is okay. Give it time, develop more, then step out and do what you need to do. Do what God leads you to do, Amen! People don't need just to HEAR the Gospel, they also need to SEE the Gospel in you.

We have this hope as an anchor for the soul, firm and secure. It enters the inner sanctuary behind the curtain,
HEBREWS 6:19 NIV

Jesus Christ is the same yesterday, today, and forever.
HEBREWS 13:8 NLT

The LORD is my rock, my fortress and my deliverer; my God is my rock, in whom I take refuge, my shield and the horn of my salvation, my stronghold.
PSALM 18:2 NIV

Break Generational Curses Before They Break You

Generational curses are rough subjects, but God delivers, and God breaks chains. Amen! First, we must learn to accept the truth so that you can cast out the lies of the enemy, and speak a different life over ourselves and our families. What your mother went through, you don't have to go through; what your father and uncle grew up doing, you don't have to do. We oversee the decisions that we make. No more excuses, no more blaming your family, no more blaming others, take responsibility and say:

I AM BETTER THAN THIS GENERATIONAL CURSE OVER MY LIFE!

Therefore we do not lose heart. Though outwardly we are wasting away, yet inwardly we are being renewed day by day. For our light and momentary troubles are achieving for us an eternal glory that far outweighs them all. So we fix our eyes not on what is seen, but on what is unseen, since what is seen is temporary, but what is unseen is eternal.
II Corinthians 4: 16-18 NIV

I may have grown up how I did, but because of God, I am not in bondage to those things anymore even though the world implies that I should be. I could not have done this by myself. God gets the glory now and forever for every area of my life and ALL the changes He has made! It is hard to live in an environment filled with fear, shame, resentment, and temptation and not be so influenced by it as to grow up and live the same way that you once despised as a child. I remember always crying when my mother smoked cigarettes. I broke her cigarettes and told her that I didn't want her to smoke.

Eventually, I grew up and started smoking. Even being a competitive athlete, I still smoked. Why? Because I was around it. My mother grew up doing it. Therefore, she did it. I grew up around it, so I allowed myself to smoke as well. See the vicious cycle that occurs? I could have refused to smoke, but instead, I allowed my flesh to get the best of me, even though I already knew what it could do. But, with God's help, I quit smoking five years ago after being a smoker for almost fifteen years. God delivered me from that, and I still thank Him each day for adding days to my life. I can be a testimony now to others that it can be done!

I remember a night that God had His angels protecting me. I borrowed my mother's car one night to go driving around. I stopped at a bar to get a drink. I was underage, but luckily the bartender was a friend of mine. I had forgotten that I had taken a pill before leaving which said on the bottle, "Do not drink alcohol." (It's called a generational curse, and that is exactly what happens to our children if we are not careful about what we do around them). Let us choose to be the example, not the problem!

I had three mixed drinks, and I got up to leave that night. I was feeling fine until I got into the car. I started to drive back to the house, which was thirty minutes away, and my vision became impaired. I start swerving off the road. I tried to slow down, but there were cars behind me. Then I started to feel sick. I started throwing up everywhere! I was still driving, mind you. I tried to find a road to stop on, but I could barely see in the dark, so I just kept driving the whole time I was throwing up. I was crying and said, "God, please get me home safely." I finally made it home, and I walked in to see my mom and stepdad (my father) standing at the door. They knew I was drunk and to top it off, I had thrown up all over my mother's car. I felt bad. I passed out on my bed but ended up waking up at three in the morning to clean out my mother's car. It was a shame that I allowed myself to do something so stupid, but these are the very things that will kill you if you don't RISE above them and say, "NO!"

I could have died that night because I chose to act foolishly, but because of God, I am here to testify and share my story with you, and hope that you will be smarter when making decisions. Don't drink and drive, but instead choose to save lives, your life and the lives of others. I could have gotten myself killed. Worse yet, I could have killed someone else, and I would have had to live with that for the rest of my life. But God made a way. We learn from each other and our failures and mistakes each day. But hey, on a positive note, now instead of drinking alcohol or whiskey, I drink that good ole Jesus Juice with a shot of the Holy Ghost on the side. If God delivered you too, SHOUT an Amen!

> *Because of the Lord's great love we are not consumed,*
> *for his compassions never fail. They are new every*
> *morning; great is your faithfulness.*
> LAMENTATIONS 3:22-23 NIV

It is time to forgive the wounded inner child within, and let God supply you with a healed inner child. You can do anything with Christ. Something I like to remember: Freedom comes with a price, but first you must find your deliverance in Christ! If you want freedom, you must first pay the price. What is your life worth to you? I could have never broken those chains that kept me in bondage all those years without the love, mercy, and power of God!

For he that is dead is freed from sin. Now if we be dead
with Christ, we believe that we shall also live with him:
ROMANS 6:7-8 KJV

Generational Curses have a huge effect on us, but we can be the difference. If God changed me and brought me out of it, He will do the same for you. He is no respecter of persons (Romans 2:11). It does not matter if the problem is drugs, alcohol, sexuality, health issues, psychological issues, or eating habits. God can change your life, and your life does not have to be the same as those who came before you. You can be the difference in your children's lives and the generations to come! You can choose not to partake of sin that get passed down from one generational to the next, but only with God's help will you succeed. Here is the Scripture to back it up!

Thou shalt not bow down thyself to them,
nor serve them: for I the LORD thy God am a jealous God,
visiting the iniquity of the fathers upon the children unto
the third and fourth generation of them that hate me;
And shewing mercy unto thousands of them that love me,
and keep my commandments.
EXODUS 20:5-6 KJV

Let go of your pride and your ego, for now is not the time to get sidetracked. Jesus is coming, and we need to be as ready as we possibly can, Amen! How can we have a voice and not use it? How can we see the world and the mess that it's in, but not take steps to do anything about it? How can we have feelings of importance and purpose deep within our souls, and be given opportunities to touch lives of and make a difference in this world, but not believe that we are good enough to do it?

There is a time for everything, and a season for every
activity under the heavens:
ECCLESIASTES 3:1 NIV

The answer to this last question is easy, the only reason you don't is because you won't! It's because someone in your life chose to continue down a sinful path that made you suffer the consequences of mental and emotional abuse. It is sad to see that it's happening all over the world. We live it every day. If the path changes course, it has got to stop in your life! Restoration then edification! Restore yourself so that you can share your testimony and help restore someone else! Discipleship and evangelism at its finest.

Return to your home, and declare how much
God has done for you...
LUKE 8:39 ESV

And they have conquered him by the blood of the Lamb and
by the word of their testimony, for they loved
not their lives even unto death.
REVELATION 12:11 ESV

So everyone who acknowledges me before men, I also will
acknowledge before my Father who is in heaven,
MATTHEW 10:32 ESV

but in your hearts honor Christ the Lord as holy, always
being prepared to make a defense to anyone who asks
you for a reason for the hope that is in you; yet do it with
gentleness and respect,
I PETER 3:15 ESV

A human mind tries to analyze what is on the inside of a box by first looking at the appearance on the outside of the box. A true Christian, walking in the Spirit of God, already knows the importance of what is on the inside first, because the outside doesn't matter. The promise is on the inside and promise comes with victory. Victory comes from God, and God restores the broken. God loves broken people because without brokenness, He could never put us back together; for if we are not broken, we cannot be fixed. Effective communication with God will result in more useful outcomes. It is important to listen for correction, apply it to your life, and react quickly. You will share the innermost parts of you with the world, so make sure God is in you, and you are in God. Don't conform to this world, but Rise Up, and fight the good fight! Don't get so caught up in the routine of the world that it causes you to backslide.

CHAPTER 5

The Backslider of Yesterday, Today, and Tomorrow

And I will restore to you the years that the locust hath eaten, the cankerworm, and the caterpiller, and the palmerworm, my great army which I sent among you. And ye shall eat in plenty, and be satisfied, and praise the name of the LORD your God, that hath dealt wondrously with you: and my people shall never be ashamed.

JOEL 2:25-26 KJV

The candle that once burned with flame has now fallen dim and become cold. Once you walked in love, but now feel nothing but bitterness, hatred, and shame. You have fallen into self-condemnation as well as put the blame on others for your fall. God can bring you out or remove you from anything.

Behold, I am the LORD, the God of all flesh. Is anything too hard for me?

JEREMIAH 32:27 ESV

I don't care what your situation was, is, or will be, God will see you through. The only reason why God would not see it through is if you don't allow Him to do what needs to be done in your life. I remember dating a boy that started using cocaine. I knew that God did not want me dating him, but I did it anyway. I recall many times him asking me if I wanted to try it and I always said, "No!" but then one day I said, "Yes." I allowed myself to give into my flesh knowing that it was wrong and knowing what it could do to me. After the first time I used cocaine, I couldn't stop. I started doing it all the time with him. Months went by, and I started noticing my life just falling apart. I didn't want to do anything but cocaine. I realized that I had become the very thing that I never wanted to be. I allowed myself to backslide and turn away from God. I stopped listening to Him, and because of that, I was paying the consequences.

There came a time when God touched me and told me that enough was enough. He spoke to my spirit and told me that I was better than that, and He had much more planned for me. He wanted me to know that I needed to quit doing what I was doing before it was too late. So, one day, I just went to my boyfriend and said, "I can no longer be with you or continue doing this to myself." I said. "NO!"

God gave me strength during a time when I was alone listening to Him which caused me to RISE and be set free from that bondage. Not only did He set me free, but I was no longer addicted. I didn't need rehab or help. He was my help, and as soon as I quit, He gave me the strength that I needed to move forward and live without it. That was one of the best decisions I ever made in my life. If I wouldn't have listened to God, I may not be here today to tell the story. Since that day, I have never done cocaine again. I thank God for saving my life that day! If He can do that for me, He will do the same for you if you let Him.

We are our own worst enemies, and at times when we backslide, we blame ourselves but have trouble forgiving ourselves. Just because someone hurts you in the church does not mean God hurt you. Just because someone you trusted lied to you doesn't mean you cannot trust God. Just because you went back to doing something that God delivered you from doesn't mean that He can't do it again. You didn't get the job you have been praying for, it's okay. God might not have wanted you to have it, or maybe you didn't get it because He has something better for you down the road. Maybe working in ministry hurts your vision because of all that you see and hear, but don't blame it on God. RISE TO THE MISSION, and be different. Be the one that RISES when others fall. Be the voice of tomorrow while everyone else is trying to be the voice of today. Bring the love of Jesus back even though others are walking in hatred and defeat. Stop allowing circumstances of life and the decisions of others to stop you from growing in Christ. People may talk about you. Who cares? They may mock you. Let them! Jesus had all of this done to Him but did He give up? NO! He kept fighting even in moments of weakness. We will never be Jesus, but we can strive to be the best we can be in Jesus, Amen!

You were running well.
Who hindered you from obeying the truth?
GALATIANS 5:7 ESV

We all have caused pain in the lives of others, but have also brought happiness to the hearts of the wounded. We can learn to change our attitudes, our actions, and our way of life at any given moment but only with God's help. There is a season for everything so if you are going through a season of fear, doubt, anger, frustration, hurt, shame, or confusion as I was when I found God, just find a comfortable place, open your heart for prayer and discuss, and give it ALL to Him! You see what happened to me, and look how far He has brought me. He will do the same for you. Your life is precious and every day you wait is a day that you leave behind and that you can't get back.

I called upon the LORD in distress:
the LORD answered me, and set me in a large place.
The LORD is on my side; I will not fear:
what can man do unto me?
PSALM 118:5-6 KJV

We see this every day: people who think that they have time to change who say, "I'll do it tomorrow." But that is the problem. "I will change when she changes and apologies." We blame others for us falling, but really it is a problem within ourselves and our relationship with God. If you allowed someone else to keep you from church, reading the Word of God, or praying, then the problem is internal. What we need to do is figure out the true reason for what has happened in our lives when we get to this place, the place that causes us to fall even though we have resources to RISE!

What if God took away your ability to see or speak? What would be your first thought? I don't think we understand the importance of our lives, our voices, our sight, our hearts, and our minds. We take for granted the very things that God gives us as gifts. If you have been delivered, stop going back! If you are currently in a battle, give it to God and ask Him to help you overcome this bondage. Ask God to strengthen you in your weakest areas, to test you when needed, and to build you with courage to face the fear and shame that has overshadowed you for long enough.

> *Cry aloud, spare not, lift up thy voice like a trumpet,*
> *and shew my people their transgression,*
> *and the house of Jacob their sins.*
> ISAIAH 58:1 KJV

> *Speak up for those who cannot speak for themselves,*
> *for the rights of all who are destitute.*
> PROVERBS 31:8 NIV

Stop walking around in self-denial, self-condemnation, and self-shame. I know that some people's situations are worse than others, but we all hurt the same! We all have the same emotions, and we feel the same way when our situation hits us individually. Don't continue to be the problem. Find the issue and deal with it right now! If it's someone in the church, talk about it and take someone with you if it doesn't get resolved the first time. If it is a family member, be real with them! Don't hide and complain but not be able to face the problem in person and fix it. So many things can be holding you back, but the real problem is you and the fact that you have held it all in; it is now holding you back from your future.

Good news, there is an answer! You don't have to stay in your current predicament, brothers and sisters. Jesus has saved you from yourself before, and He will do it again! He loves you as much right now than He did years ago, or even months ago. Rise to the Mission in loving yourself and others again, develop yourself and find out who you truly are in Christ, and then go out and be an example of His love and mercy! You are not the only one going through hard times and circumstances. So many others are hurting and do not know what to do. Be there for them, encourage them, but don't force it. Allow people to come to the Lord themselves, and with the right heart. As for you, forgive others and forgive yourself. We repent when we sin, and we fall short of the glory of God daily whether we realize it or not. Stop allowing the enemy to hold you where you are, wipe that dust off and get back to business in Jesus Name!

> *Wake up, and strengthen what remains*
> *and is about to die, for I have not found your works*
> *complete in the sight of my God.*
> REVELATION 3:2 ESV

No matter how many years go by, there will always be backsliders. It's unfortunate, but people lose focus on who the relationship is with and they lose their passion. Are you in a relationship with Jesus or in the hands of others pretending to be God who have taken your life and made it their own? Never give others that much power over your life. When you start getting sucked into that, it is time to let go! Love them, but know your worth, Amen! We wouldn't go to church if we didn't need help, so no more excuses on being a sinner and not wanting to be a hypocrite in the church either. We all have issues that we are facing, but our job is to continue seeking God and staying grounded in Him. Your roots should grow so tall and so strong that they wrap around the cross and can never be moved.

You are the salt of the earth, but if salt has lost its taste,
how shall its saltiness be restored? It is no longer
good for anything except to be thrown out
and trampled under people's feet.
MATTHEW 5:13 ESV

Grow in knowledge, be stronger than your situation, and RISE TO THE MISSION again to be all that God has created you to be. Do this with the heart of Jesus, and always do everything in Jesus Name!

Set Me Free From These Prison Walls

For a backslider, learning to live again is a hard process. You feel like a prisoner behind bars with a life sentence and the possibility of never getting out. I remember how hard it was for me to get back on track after continuing to backslide. Luckily my daughter's father was in church and got me going back to church when we first started dating. I started looking to Jesus again. After that God just really took charge of my life and has completely turned it around. Thank you, Clarence, for helping me get back on track. I will always be grateful for what you did for me.

I don't know what happened in between me being saved as a child and before I asked God for forgiveness again, but I got off track. I started hanging out with the wrong people, listening to the wrong things, and allowing the enemy to make a fool out of me. I had to make decisions that I never thought I would have to because of my selfish actions, and now I will forever pay for them, but I do not have to allow them to control me, and I don't. God forgave me when I recommitted my life to Him after all those years of living in sin, and He blessed me with the gift of the Holy Ghost with evidence of speaking in tongues. It was my time to receive. When I put my faith back into Him, He put His faith back into me! I will always be thankful.

You never know who God will place in your life for your season of development and change. Therefore, respect everyone and love all of those who God puts in your life, whether it be for a short time or your whole life.

When you first decide to return to the same sin that God brought you out of, you feel weak and defeated, but God is a God of mercy and the God of second chances. He knows you're hurting and lost, but He also knows your heart, your intentions, and He knows your thoughts. You cannot fool God, you may fool others, but God is always watching and always listening. It is vital for your present and future life to have *living* in it as much as possible. I'm talking about living each day with joy in your heart for God, and a mission in mind! I say this every day,

"God, send me someone today to bring forth into the Kingdom of God" or "Lord, I ask you to walk before me in all that I do and to bring me someone who needs your Word today."

God can and will heal you, deliver you, break the chains of bondage that hold you hostage by the enemy, cause breakthrough in your life, bring peace over your mind even in the worst of times, and restore you back to even better than before. Rise to the Mission Backslider! No matter why you have chosen to fall short, no matter how long you have felt like this isn't for you, RISE TO THE MISSION and repent. You no longer have to be stuck! You no longer must live the way that you're living. Make the declaration today, "I am no longer lost in Christ, but am found with more purpose, love, and worth than ever before." Jesus has never left you and He never will, but He chose to allow you to have time to think and act. Preparation for your mission to come. If you rise above this and accept who you are and what your purpose is, God will prepare a way for you and will always give you what you need to grow and learn in Him.

By staying in sin, your light has become shaded, but luckily is not faded. Somewhere deep inside is the memory of freedom from your thoughts, the thoughts of others, and the voices of fear that never seem to leave you for long. You may feel chained in bondage to your sin, but you carry the truth inside, and it hurts to know you are outside God's will. Maybe someone has hurt you (even someone from church), or maybe you have hurt yourself with your bad choices. Others may have you bound and broken, may be abusing you mentally, physically, or sexually. You may want to fall apart, but don't! RISE to the occasion and lean on God for deliverance from the sin, the abuse, and the situation.

We have the God of all mercy and grace in our midst. Choose to have a relationship with Him even though you may not be able to smile or taste His goodness right now. Jesus is in you and is ready for you to Rise to the Mission. Come forth again. Put the things that have brought you to this place on the shelf. Remember who you are in Christ and be free.

Fly like an eagle that has just been set free from his cage, and to freedom, it shall stay. Embrace the new adventure ahead that will never be led by your weaknesses, but by His strength found in you. Face your fears for they are your strengths for tomorrow. Face the fake, for that is when you find what is real. Face criticism, for that is what brings growth and maturity. Face those who talk about you, for Jesus said it would come, and when it does come, know that you are doing something right! Rise up, people of God and break through this wall that has been self-built only to protect you. Who is it really hurting though? Shine again for all to see for your pain shall be taken away. Down an open road you shall go without putting on a show. So, those who are NOW in the same situation you WERE in can see the Risen Soul and glorify the Father.

The rising of the fallen soul shall bring forth more fruit now than ever before. The Lord loves you now and forever more. His blood shall cover, strengthen, and encourage you. For the Lord, thy God is with thee now and forever. No matter your situation, God hears your cries. He wipes the tears from your eyes, and He never says goodbye. This time is just a season and a reason to watch and listen, and to bring feeling, emotion, and experience into the mix. He has brought you up for such a time as this!

For if thou altogether holdest thy peace at this time,
then shall there enlargement and deliverance arise to the
Jews from another place; but thou and thy father's house
shall be destroyed: and who knoweth whether thou art
come to the kingdom for such a time as this?
ESTHER 4:14 KJV

Do you feel like you have failed life miserably on your own? You often wonder if this is as good as it can get. Is this all there is to life?

Is there even more out there for someone like you? If you are someone who can relate with me on these things, I can say in all honesty that I was there. I know exactly how you feel. You may feel as though you have gotten off track, but I can assure you, Jesus will show you the way if you allow Him. All you must do is ask for His help. It is hard to deal with negatives feelings and emotions by yourself. Jesus is ready to restore you and make changes in your life even at this very moment. He wants to heal your body and deliver you from the things of this world. He wants to bring peace over your mind and solitude to your heart even from past abuse. God always wants the best for you. No matter who you are right now, by the time you finish this book, I pray that God touches your heart and that you will draw closer to forming a relationship with Him.

God is there to stand in your defense during your struggle. He never forces you but gives you free will to choose if you want to have Him lead your life or if you want to lead you own life. If you continue fighting God, then you could lose this fight that you were never meant to lose! Therefore, it's time to give up those gloves! If you want to walk with God, it is time to give up the pride, walk in faith, learn to use God's Holy Word in your life, and stand firm on His promises! If you don't know His promises, get out your Bible and search them! Have the kind of faith that brings victory at the sound of the bell. Never count yourself out, just count yourself ABLE!

Now is a time to love again, to discover who you are, and to proclaim your victory in Jesus Christ. Rise to the Mission, the mission from the original dreamer who brings life after death, healing after disease, and deliverance to the sinner. The Rising of Jesus is the reason for your mission. Too many are sleeping and need to be woke up. Too many of are hurting and need to be restored. Too many are walking in self-righteousness because of lack of humility. Too many are sitting in condemnation of themselves when really, they should be exalting the Father in Heaven. You are allowing the enemy to overtake your thoughts. He is turning your situation around on you so that you don't think you are worthy to Rise Up and conquer this situation. But let me tell you something: He is wrong! It is about you and God, not you and other people. It is about you picking up right where you left off and never turning back again. You don't have to start completely over. Just ask God, right now, to shake your spirit and stir your mind!

God already gave you what you needed to maintain while you were figuring things out. Allow God to speak to you and lead you from right where you are. Learn to live again and when you learn to live, walk your walk in love and faith in our Lord and Savior.

> *And walk in love, as Christ also hath loved us,*
> *and hath given himself for us an offering and a sacrifice to*
> *God for a sweetsmelling savour.*
> EPHESIANS 5:2 KJV

God does not have a limit. Therefore, we do not have a limit! When you decide to give your life to God, all that is within you that is dead or causing you pain, hurt, oppression, or depression, must die and be given to God. That means you must first know what these things are, accept that they are hurting you, and ask God to get rid of them. God will start the formation (process) when you start your walk with Him. If you are an alcoholic, the Holy Spirit will start convicting you which means you will get an anxious feeling that something is not quite right every time you go to take a swig. Then when change happens, God will get the glory! God will also place it upon your heart that what you are doing is not pleasing to Him and He will let you know that it is something that will hurt you. You will feel it in your gut.

I remember as I got older and started doing things I wasn't supposed to do that God let me know that I was not doing the right things. When you don't know right from wrong, it is understandable, but when you know right and don't do right, He will let you know for sure. Nothing gets past Him. I always say to my children, "I have eyes in the back of my head." Well, God has eyes everywhere! God is not the author of confusion, but is the God of peace! So, if you keep selling drugs, the Holy Spirit will let you know that it's not in God's will to do so. The wonderful thing about God is that He will stop the things in you that are of the world so that He can replace those things with the image and character of Himself.

And when he is come, he will reprove the world of sin,
and of righteousness, and of judgment: Of sin, because
they believe not on me; Of righteousness, because I go to
my Father, and ye see me no more; Of judgment,
because the prince of this world is judged.
JOHN 16:8-11 KJV

I stand firm in the promises of God because His Word has never let me down, and He showed me that He wouldn't let me down in my walk with Him either. He is not someone who just says something and doesn't do it; He shows you who He is through His actions. It didn't happen overnight, but I grew to trust Him. If I knew then what I know now, I would not be the person I am today. I would be better and further along in my Christian walk. Others may have let me down, I may let myself down at times, but God's Word never changes, unlike this world which is ever-changing. God also provides you with a mantle for your mission. Your mantle is the tool needed to move you to the next level.

For the word of the Lord is right and true;
he is faithful in all he does. The Lord loves righteousness
and justice; the earth is full of his unfailing love.
By the word of the Lord the heavens were made,
their starry host by the breath of his mouth.
PSALM 33:4-6 NIV

CHAPTER 6

Mantle for The Mission

So Elijah went from there and found Elisha son of Shaphat.
He was plowing with twelve yoke of oxen, and he himself
was driving the twelfth pair. Elijah went up to him and
threw his cloak around him. Elisha then left his oxen
and ran after Elijah. "Let me kiss my father and mother
goodbye," he said, "and then I will come with you."...
I KINGS 19:19-20 NIV

Your cloak is your mantle (covering), and it is your gift from God. It stands for the call that you have over your life that God gave you. Your mantle has purpose and you must find that purpose. *Purpose* is a strong word now so don't go getting antsy on me. Just do some research, study, reflect, and ask God to show you how to give meaning and wholeness to your life and the lives of others while He uses you. Pray for discernment. Be honest with yourself and understand that you don't know everything. Look inside the looking glass and notice the mirror in which you carry! It took me a while to realize that I wasn't Little Miss Know-It-All. That comes with maturity, but we all realize it at different levels. If you truly want change, you will seek to find the answers just as a student in a classroom trying to remember the answer to the question on the study guide. The student gets out his textbook and looks through the book until he finds the answer. It is the same with God. He has given us the Holy Bible to be our study guide and answer key through the best of times and the darkest of times. The Bible is the key to understanding life, your purpose, and what God's plans are for your life. I knew I was supposed to step out into the world and discover who I was and what my purpose was, but I had no idea where to start. Then I learned that it doesn't happen with a blink of an eye, but it happens as we get closer to God.

After finding your purpose, it is also important to help the next generation find their purpose. Understand the importance of the youth! They are our future leaders. Children do not just learn from us, we learn from them too. We need to lay out a foundation for them so that they have what they need to be all that they can be with God. We learn from our elders, and they are also learning constantly from us. Have more compassion about the next generations coming up. Instead of talking about how different they are from your generation, find ways to teach them and lift their heads to God and not force them to walk the streets because you stick your nose up at them. The roads less traveled will be their pathway due to their upbringing. Prepare a way so that they can live to tell their story that God has prepared for them, as He has prepared for you and me.

There is a poem that I truly enjoy, and will always remain hidden in my heart. It is called:

The Bridge Builder
by Will Allen Dromgoole.

An old man, going a lone highway,
Came at the evening cold and gray
To a chasm vast and deep and wide
Through which was flowing a swollen tide.
The old man crossed in the twilight dim;
The rapids held no fears for him.
But he turned when safe on the other side
And built a bridge to span the tide.

"Old man," cried a fellow pilgrim near,
"You're wasting your time in building here.
Your journey will end with the closing day;
You never again will pass this way.
You have crossed the chasm deep and wide;
Why build you this bridge at even-tide?"

The builder lifted his old gray head.
"Good friend, in the path I have come," he said,
"There follows after me today
A youth whose feet must pass this way.
This stream, which has been as naught to me,
To that fair youth may a pitfall be.
He too must cross in the twilight dim —
Good friend, I am building this bridge for him."

There is a covenant within us. When all seems lost, when others see the negative and look at the actions of the person or outward appearance of man, a Godly mind looks inward and sees what could be. God always shows us the future and not the present. Just like we look at a child or those that are young adults. We learn to follow as children so that we can lead as adults. Your actions can change a child's life. How you treat children can change their attitudes. Time spent with them and encouraging them can shift their focus on becoming more than they could ever dream. Help our children become future leaders with a voice and a mission. Help them RISE UP and make a difference. I see something beautiful in each one of the children that I have the opportunity to meet. To have the heart of a child is the most amazing gift and to have the mind of a teenager or young adult is a powerful weapon as well.

Now is a time when a student mentality is needed. Always be willing to learn from others and teach others what you know. What use is what you know if you are not sharing it with the world? It is our jobs to care enough about the future of our youth to step up and love them and help them succeed in every way we can, both in the home and in the community. Pick up your mantle young man or young woman, choose to Rise Above the things of this world and live a life filled with knowledge, growth, and purpose. Stop hiding in the bushes and start a fire within your soul! Pick up your mantle, brother and sister, and allow God to give you all that you need to be successful in your calling. He is speaking to you; don't ignore His grace for you never know when He will give it to another and take it away from you.

The Hope That Holds Your Future

When we reflect on the heart of God, we see the beauty in things that others don't see. We recognize life, promise, and change in the parts of the world and individuals that tend to go unnoticed. There are moments that we just never want to let go of. Moments that warm our heart and bring tears to our eyes. Moments that stop us in our tracks and take us deep into our hearts desires and comforts us beyond measure.

I can remember one night, not long ago when my six-year-old daughter wrapped her precious little arms around me and said, "Mom, I am going to pray that tomorrow will be better for you." She said this calmly and with much sincerity in her heart. She knew Momma needed to take a deep breath, and like God, she wanted to give me just what I needed to calm my storm. God did that for me through her. That is hope! That is joy! That is love! That is peace! What blessed me in that time of love and comfort was that she came to pray for me! One of the most important things to me is that my children know God, know who they are in Christ, and the importance of their faith which brings forth prayer. God was using my daughter to let me know that He was with me.

Another time when God let me know to keep my hope alive and that He had not forgotten about me was when Aiden and I had a discussion outside laying down while looking at the stars. Aiden started saying how beautiful the stars were and how bright they are at night, and I remember telling him that they were our dreams and purpose. The stars represented all the dreams of the people here on earth, and that every time we look up at them, if one shines extra bright, then that star was ours. Aiden smiled and said, "Mom, God made those stars to shine bright for us always to let us know that He is watching over us and giving us light even in the darkness." That made me really tear up. That was a very special moment between a mother and a son which I will always cherish. So, whether we have our rainy days today or our winter flurries tomorrow, God always reminds us that He is there in whatever falls or rises in our lives. He is with us! His All-Surpassing Power never fails us!

But we have this treasure in earthen vessels, that the excellency of the power may be of God, and not of us.
II CORINTHIANS 4:7 KJV

Your mantle will bring forth faith that will overcome the world one step at a time. With each step brings a new beginning for the life of another soul. Understanding will come later, but knowing your purpose and walking in faith will bring wisdom to your mind and understanding in your spirit. God places individuals in our lives to help us understand.

Continue to have faith in God. He is the only hope for your future! Watch your future and the lives of others come alive when you find your freedom on the rock.

At first, seeing is not always believing. Things can appear harder than what they are, or someone may give the wrong impression at first, but on the inside, they may be completely different than what you see. There is a journey that we must take. It's your faith that leads you to your destination and to loving others for who they are, and even loving yourself for who you are. After you have reached your mark, done the impossible, seen yourself make it to where you never thought you could, or seen your mentality totally shift, that my friend, is when you see your mantle in action.

It's is important to remember that even though God wants to bless us abundantly, we may not be ready for all that He has planned for us. As we grow and continue to submit to Him, we will advance to a higher level. That is when fulfillment occurs. We can't continue to stay where we are. Change is hard, but change is good. We need to push ourselves to grow individually, to become wiser in our walk with God. It is our responsibility to listen to God and to do the right thing in all we do. We don't always do right in God's eyes, but we can strive to do our best. It's a process. Continue to tell yourself who you are in Christ. You will hit some speed bumps, you might even fall off track, but God always works it out. We are blessed and rewarded when we remain faithful. Be devoted and filled with hope in your heavenly Father and He will make a way even when there seems to be no way. Allow Him to lead you to the everlasting freedom that you long for. Keep that fire burning within your soul, and He will give you the desires of your heart.

Now unto him that is able to do exceeding abundantly above all that we ask or think, according to the power that worketh in us, Unto him be glory in the church by Christ Jesus throughout all ages, world without end. Amen.
Ephesians 3:20-21 KJV

Blessed are the pure in heart, for they shall see God.
Matthew 5:8 ESV

Commit thy way unto the LORD; trust also in him;
and he shall bring it to pass. And he shall bring forth
thy righteousness as the light, and thy judgment as the
noonday. Rest in the LORD, and wait patiently for him…
PSALM 37:5-7 KJV

Think about your development goals and what God is asking of you. Think about what hinders you from progressing in your walk with God and change it. Think about how you can overcome the obstacles now and in the future. Think about coming up with a plan of how you will know when and if you're making progress in growing spiritually within yourself and helping others grow as well. It is time to act, not just spiritually, but mentally, emotionally, and physically as well. Take care of all aspects of your life, and watch God cause you to RISE TO THE MISSION in each one of them. You will look back and say, "Look what I accomplished with God on my side." If you are curious, then pursue it. Be well rounded and start learning new things. The more you know, the more valuable you are in the Body of Christ. Ask for bigger, and bigger shall be given to you, Amen! Always think through your actions as well because your decisions today will have consequences tomorrow. Make your decisions count where they are needed; and needed where they count! God owns our hearts, and in Him, our happiness remains. Always keep this a focus point and learn to LOVE as He loves.

CHAPTER 7

The Love that Heals Our Past, Present, and Future

*But God, who is rich in mercy, for his great love wherewith
he loved us, Even when we were dead in sins, hath
quickened us together with Christ, (by grace ye are saved;)*
EPHESIANS 2:4-5 KJV

Take a deep breath and thank God for allowing you to come to terms with forgiveness, and giving you this new strength to walk with more love and compassion for yourself and others. Forgiveness is a very important step on your journey with God, but after you get through that, now it is time to learn how to love yourself as God loves you. See your heart as His heart. See your hands as His hands. Soar on the breath of His Word as He carries you on His shoulders! You cannot pour God's love all over the world if you do not first love yourself. Without love in your heart for yourself, you cannot truly love others.

*To acquire wisdom is to love yourself;
people who cherish understanding will prosper.*
PROVERBS 19:8 NLT

Love does not come easy if you have been hurt, especially by the ones you love the most. No one can hurt you like a family member or someone you love dearly. Always remember, the strength that you carry within yourself is far more valuable than the body in which you protect it with! I want you to imagine yourself walking along the beach, barefoot at sunset, sun shining down on your face, and the wind blowing through your hair as you take a deep breath of the fresh ocean scent, only to come across a message in a bottle. Before picking the bottle up, you start to wonder if what is inside the bottle is going to be of some help to you. Notice that you are more interested in what is inside the bottle than the bottle itself.

God cares more about your heart than He does your past. God cares more about you than He does your setbacks. Your past does not define who you are anymore but merely helps give meaning to your future, just as you should not judge someone else from their outward appearance or their past. God uses us all! Your blessings will fit where your soul is, and they will also fit the size of your heart. If your heart is not ready to receive, He will not give them. If your soul is not where it should be, you could be missing out on your "on time" blessing. Be open to loving others and be open to change no matter how comfortable or uncomfortable you are. God will not give you something that your heart can't handle. He knows your intentions, and if you will appreciate what He does for you, He knows others will appreciate what you do for them!

When you are made free from sin and give your life to God, you will have freedom which brings forth love, the Love of Christ.

But now being made free from sin, and become servants to
God, ye have your fruit unto holiness,
and the end everlasting life.
Romans 6:22 KJV

I have never been perfect. I was born in sin the very first day. I lived in fear before knowing the Lord, and I never knew myself to love myself. BUT WITH GOD: I am still not perfect, but I improve each day. I have been forgiven for my sins, and the chains of multiple bondages I was in were broken. Now I live each day in His Word! I no longer live in fear because God has provided in me a sound mind, courage, and strength. It is His power that sustains me, but most importantly, I now understand who I am and what my purpose is. I love myself because Jesus loves me and sees me worthy to be loved, just as He does you!

For I know the thoughts that I think toward you,
saith the LORD, thoughts of peace, and not of evil,
to give you an expected end.
JEREMIAH 29:11 KJV

But God commendeth his love toward us, in that,
while we were yet sinners, Christ died for us.
ROMANS 5:8 KJV

I will praise the Lord no matter what happens. I will
constantly speak of his glories and grace. I will boast of all
his kindness to me. Let all who are discouraged take heart.
Let us praise the Lord together and exalt his name.
PSALM 34:1-3 TLB

Don't allow the enemy to rob you of your blessing no matter how big or small, stay focused on God! He will bless you in accordance to your faithfulness and obedience, but He won't give you everything at once. Every so often He will give you more and more and more. When Kyleigh was trying to learn how to walk or use the toilet for the first time, she got personal one-on-one time with her father and me to teach her to walk by herself and use the toilet by herself. Then she was given an opportunity to show us that she was learning and paying attention or listening to us. Then after much practice and obeying the instructions she was given, Kyleigh finally took those first few steps and was able to use the toilet by herself. That is how our walk with God is, steady and constant. You and your Father in Heaven form a special bond based on reciprocal love. How can you love God with all your heart if you can't even love yourself? You can't.

Your broken heart does not have to remain shattered and empty! God restores you and sustains you for what your future holds. Even before coming to Christ, He puts treasure within you that manifests after you come to a saving knowledge of Christ.

And I will give thee the treasures of darkness,
and hidden riches of secret places, that thou mayest know
that I, the LORD, which call thee by thy name,
am the God of Israel.
ISAIAH 45:3 KJV

I have always had a good heart, but didn't love myself. I always looked to others, especially men, for attention. That was because I longed for the right love that I never got from my father. It's time to take your mind out of the situation you're in and just give all your thoughts, emotions, hurt, and pain to God. I didn't know God then like I do now. I didn't know what to do or how to start. How do I start to love myself? I asked myself that question many times. Every situation is different, but first, you really need to admit that you don't love yourself. You have to make a commitment to take steps to love yourself again. God has your back, Jesus has your back, and the Holy Spirit has your back. All are part of the triune Godhead, but all do different things for you and help you in different ways so that you have every resource needed to succeed. After a while, your relationship with the Father, the Son, and the Holy Spirit lead to a successful future with love all around you.

For now we see only a reflection as in a mirror;
then we shall see face to face. Now I know in part;
then I shall know fully, even as I am fully known.
I CORINTHIANS 13:12 NIV

There is a starting point for all of us, but God wants you to push on the gas with some self-esteem, worth, and faith and He will get you to the finish line! It might help to pretend that the person you want to tell you that you are beautiful is standing in front of you until you feel beautiful. You tell that person, "From this day forward I am going to be beautiful for me, and not for you!

For freedom Christ has set us free; stand firm therefore,
and do not submit again to a yoke of slavery.
GALATIANS 5:1 ESV

Love is in the eye of the beholder. When you look at others, do you look with your own eyes or with the eyes of Jesus? No matter which direction you take, if you walk in love you walk in everything you need. This, brothers and sisters, is the Jesus kind of love! The love without limits. The kind of love that would die for you even though you would not die for it. God shows us His love every day. The very breath that you take is a sign of His love for without it, you could not truly appreciate the good from the bad, the smiles from the tears, the courage while afraid, the hope even during failure, or the darkness you face each day. Jesus' love is the true love we need.

For I am persuaded, that neither death, nor life,
nor angels, nor principalities, nor powers, nor things
present, nor things to come, Nor height, nor depth, nor any
other creature, shall be able to separate us from the love of
God, which is in Christ Jesus our Lord.
ROMANS 8:38-39 KJV

When I didn't have a father in my life, He was my father. When I didn't have a friend, He was my friend and has remained my friend to this day. My best friend! When I need guidance, He is my guidance counselor. When I have financial difficulty, He is my provider. When I need shelter, He is my source and comforter. Why? Because He loves me just like He loves you, and with that love He carries me. Day by day, hour by hour, and minute by minute, His love is yours, and His love is always in the world He created. Therefore, God needs you to love His creation and the people in it, which includes yourself. Race, religion, and gender don't matter, He loves us all! We are all precious to Him and equal in His eyes. We all serve a purpose, and He died so that we may have life and have it more abundantly, Amen!

By whom also we have access by faith into this grace wherein we stand, and rejoice in hope of the glory of God. And not only so, but we glory in tribulations also: knowing that tribulation worketh patience; And patience, experience; and experience, hope: And hope maketh not ashamed; because the love of God is shed abroad in our hearts by the Holy Ghost which is given unto us. For when we were yet without strength, in due time Christ died for the ungodly.
ROMANS 5:2-6 KJV

Jesus died for the ungodly which means that no matter what you have done, God chooses to love you. I stand before you today a changed woman because I put my faith in God and said, "God, because you love me, I will forgive myself for the things that I have done, and I will learn to love myself again."

I admit, after I became a teenager, I started getting off track. I started hanging out with the wrong people, doing drugs, smoking, drinking, partying, showing parts of my body that did not need to be shown to others, and I even experimented with bisexuality in high school. I didn't think God would forgive me for those things, but I thank Him every day for doing so. I thank God that I follow the Word of God now, and with His help, turned from that lifestyle. If He had not saved me, there is no telling where I would be or if I would even be here today. There are plenty of other things I could list that I have done, but you get my point. If you are feeling unworthy because of your thoughts, deeds, attitudes, and behaviors, remember that you ARE worthy in God's eyes. If you feel that you cannot be loved because no one ever loved you, God has always loved you and is wrapping His loving arms around you at this very moment. The lost will forever be lost in their own eyes, but in God's eyes, they are always found! God knows where you are, what you think, what you will do tomorrow, and most importantly, He knows your heart. After all, Jesus did die so that your heart and soul could have eternal life with Him in Heaven.

Happiness is not in the multitude of things but is an emotion that is birthed from compassion and love. I used to live mostly in fear, but God has helped me overcome that to some degree, and I did long for God before finding Him. I first had to want to love myself to find Him. Once I found Him, I found peace within my heart and was more gracious towards others and more receptive to Him. I had to think about my identity in Christ which was very important then, and will always be important in my walk with God. Your identity matters!

by which he has granted to us his precious and very great promises, so that through them you may become partakers of the divine nature, having escaped from the corruption that is in the world because of sinful desire.
II Peter 1:4 ESV

Some people can walk with an identity crisis, but when you are living for God, you must find your identity. Many people don't realize the impact they can have for the Kingdom when they walk boldly in their Christian identity so overlook small meaningful gestures they could perform that would mean the world to someone struggling. God wants you to try to find the answers to your life's most difficult questions. I have always been a dreamer and not just a dreamer of the future, but I would have dreams of the present that would stay with me over the years, but I never knew what they meant. I remember as a child I would tell my mother about my dreams and she would say, "Amber, you need to write a book about those dreams. It would make for a great story." She said that to me so many times that I started making notes of my dreams.

Soon my notes became poems, and after writing several, I decided to share one in a contest while I was in high school. I did not win the contest, but I did receive the Editor's Choice Award for outstanding achievement in poetry from the International Library of Poetry. That helped on my journey to understanding my gifts. Look for those kinds of clues to your gifts. Something will happen in a period when you need it the most that will show you that God has your best interest at heart. Pay attention to what God is telling you. Have your listening ears on because you could miss your special moment of truth with none other than your own personal caregiver of your future.

After receiving the poetry award, I knew that my heart was given to me for a reason and that my dreams were not just dreams, but a light from God giving me a little insight to my future!

Now the God of peace, that brought again from the dead our Lord Jesus, that great shepherd of the sheep, through the blood of the everlasting covenant, Make you perfect in every good work to do his will, working in you that which is wellpleasing in his sight, through Jesus Christ; to whom beglory for ever and ever. Amen.
HEBREWS 13:20-21 KJV

At the time I wrote the poem below, I was lost and looking for love and comfort from others, hoping that one day I would find a man who would love me the way I needed to be loved. I now realize that the love I longed for was already found in Jesus Christ.

The LORD appeared to him from afar, saying, "I have loved you with an everlasting love; Therefore I have drawn you with lovingkindness.
JEREMIAH 31:3 NEW AMERICAN STANDARD 1977

My Heart Is Open
By Amber M. Brown

No longer does my heart need to be closed. No longer does an open casket need to be aroused. My heart is open for all to see and my heart shall go to the person that shall be. The blood that flows through my body, the happiness my heart shall feel, the hole that will be open to a real, but honest soul. The key to my heart will be unlocked, to wait for an amazing shock, of love that waits for thee to be all I need but not a fee. Tenderly beating as I lay awake, taking breathes of an honest quake. The person inside of me will be the person I hope soon to be. Readied in the eye of the beholder, the heart will always be open to a contender.

You Are Stronger Than Your Situation

To exercise does not just refer to physical health, but is also useful in our mental stature as well. What use are we to ourselves and others if we are not mentally healthy? God gives us a sound mind for a reason. We walk each day with one view of ourselves and what we want to be and another of who we really are. Sometimes this gets flip flopped. Who we really are is not who we are looking at in the mirror. So, who are you really? Who are you in Christ? If you can't answer these questions, then it's time to find out! Don't let others tell you who they think you are, but find out for yourself.

Wherefore gird up the loins of your mind, be sober,
and hope to the end for the grace that is to be brought unto
you at the revelation of Jesus Christ;
I Peter 1:13 KJV

When you choose God, you will lose people. But even if you are left with only God to help you learn about yourself and your future, you still got to keep the best part and the most important piece of you and to the puzzle of life. You may lose something that you think means a lot now, but you will gain much more! Focus on less fear and more courage. You are important, you are beautiful, you are smart, you are gifted, and you are mandatory in the Body of Christ! God needs you, the world needs you, and most importantly you need yourself! When you stand firm in the promises of God, and He will make a way.

If you allow others to dictate your life, you will realize down the road how much you lost of yourself by living for someone else. Some people will understand you and some won't, but that is okay. Pick yourself up today and start walking in confidence.

If you keep my commands, you will remain in my love,
just as I have kept my Father's commands and remain in
his love. I have told you this so that my joy may be in you
and that your joy may be complete. My command is this:
Love each other as I have loved you.
John 15:10-12 NIV

Find yourself, love yourself, and stay connected to the strength within you. You will never regret changing your life for the better; the only thing you will ever regret is never getting up to do it! If you never make the first move, more than likely things will not turn out how you want them to because you started anything for it to have the chance to work out. Nothing ventured, nothing gained. Today you take those *shoulda, coulda, wouldas* and put them on the shelf forever where they belong. Let the dust hide them so that they are never touched again. You are going to accomplish all that God has for you. He is just waiting for you. Always remember that we influence others so if we get up and show people that God's strength gets us through any battle of our life, then others will see how good God is and maybe souls will be saved because of your actions. Jesus shown through us is also important on the job, in school, in the community, and in many other areas of our lives. Be a positive influence now that you are a new creature in Christ. Be the best you right now and let God show you who you are meant to be as you continue on your mission!

> *Whether you turn to the right or to the left,*
> *your ears will hear a voice behind you, saying,*
> *"This is the way; walk in it."*
> ISAIAH 30:21 NIV

Rise to the Mission and walk in God's way for your life!

RISE TO THE MISSION brothers and sisters! Your mind can be your weapon of defense, or it can be your kryptonite. You are the only one who has control over the way you think. I like to think of it as deception from the enemy. He wants to get you vulnerable and bring deception into your mind, but it's because of ignorance. The only way to stop the enemy from attacking you is to fight him with Scripture. Knowing the Word of God saves you. Scripture is the breath of God. Therefore, it has the power to destroy any plots or plans of the enemy.

> *The thief comes only to steal and kill and destroy; I have*
> *come that they may have life, and have it to the full.*
> JOHN 10:10 NIV

It is easy to use unplanned situations or unnecessary delays as an excuse to give up or think that what you want is meant for someone else, but you are worth what God has for you! Choose to think differently and to learn who you are and what you were meant to do. Sometimes we are just not ready for the things that we want. We may want them, but wanting and needing are two different things.

> *And my God will supply every need of yours according to his riches in glory in Christ Jesus.*
> PHILIPPINES 4:19 ESV

Make the choice to speak life into your surroundings and create positive thinking. Something that I always say and hold close to my heart is that creating positive thinking will bring forth positive change! If God ordained it, then no one can take it away from you. If someone in your life seems to be the reason why you are moving forward, just remember God placed him or her in your life, and He can place someone else in your life just as easily. No one person holds the key to your future. God is the only one who holds the key to your future. He just uses human vessels as helpers along the way.

> *Put on the whole armor of God, that you may be able to stand against the schemes of the devil.*
> EPHESIANS 6:11 ESV

The devil is the source of our problems. If we take out the enemy, we take out the source. How do we take out the enemy? Well, we start by loving ourselves enough to learn the Word of God, and any time the enemy starts attacking, we start speaking Scripture into the atmosphere.

> *Be sober-minded; be watchful. Your adversary the devil prowls around like a roaring lion, seeking someone to devour.*
> I PETER 5:8 ESV

Fight off the spirit of the enemy with God's Word, and then you give it to God while you are still praying. Don't stop praying. Even when He fixes your situation, keep praying, Amen! Your power is in your mouth, and the mouth of the beholder is the Lord Jesus Christ.

> *No weapon that is formed against thee shall prosper;*
> *and every tongue that shall rise against thee in judgment*
> *thou shalt condemn. This is the heritage of the servants of*
> *the LORD, and their righteousness is of me,*
> *saith the LORD.*
> Isaiah 54:17 KJV

Always keep in mind that we wouldn't be here without the Father, we wouldn't have salvation without Jesus Christ, and we wouldn't have guidance and direction without the Holy Spirit. God loves you, and now it is time to love yourself. RISE and walk in the same love that once died for you. His love won't hold you back, and will teach others about love as they watch you. Be the example and the answer, not the problem. ENCOURAGE, don't tear down.

CHAPTER 8

Parakaleo: Be a Light to Those in Darkness

For you were once darkness, but now you are light in the Lord. Live as children of light
EPHESIANS 5:8 NIV

F or those of you who do not know what *parakaleo* means, it is a Greek verb appearing in the New Testament 110 times and means to encourage, to comfort, to call, or to summon. God wants us to shine brightly so that even those people in the lowest of places notice us! Do not be of the world, but break through the world, Amen. Reach people where they are, not where you think they should be. Show God's love when spreading the Gospel. What do you do when darkness is your natural reality and freedom hasn't found you yet? I came across this Scripture as I was studying the Word of God and it reads,

Knowing this, that our old man is crucified with him, that the body of sin might be destroyed, that henceforth we should not serve sin.
ROMANS 6:6 KJV

That really hit me and made me realize that now that I was set free from my sins, I could never go back again. To know who I am in Christ and to live as a child of the living God is one of the greatest revelations I could ever have.

We are continuously trying to learn how to live for God and how not to live for the world. Death can come upon us at any moment, and something deadly in life can come upon at the worst possible time. The Word of God is necessary in our everyday life. As soon as we get God's Word placed in our hearts, the enemy tries to come and take it. For example, we can hear or read about loving others and not fighting. We can learn to how to compromise and not complain. But as soon we arrive at work, we get into an argument with someone or start complaining about the car troubles we had on the way. These are the kinds of plots and plans that the enemy uses to get us sidetracked so that the Word we just heard will be forgotten. The enemy doesn't want you keeping God's precious and Holy Word within your hearts and letting it conform you and mold you to be more like Jesus, so he sabotages you every time you let him.

I have fallen into this pattern many times. I have heard a good Word, received revelation on it, but did not let it sink in my heart and stay there. I allowed the enemy to make me doubt my capabilities and worth and I forgot who I was in Christ. That slowed me down along my walk in growing as a daughter of Christ and learning, but quickly Jesus rescued me again. He only rescued me because I realized what was happening and started taking action! God doesn't do all the work. We must get up and act as well. In Exodus 14, God told Moses to hold out his hand over the Red Sea and God caused a strong east wind to part the waters so that the Israelites could go across on dry land. God gave the command and Moses had to get up and act. By doing so, Moses led his people out of Egyptian bondage and toward the Promised Land. That trip should have taken eleven days, not forty years! The Hebrews allowed murmuring, grumbling, lack of faith, and doubt to keep them going around in circles until a whole generation died. Then God used Joshua and Caleb to finish Moses' mission and take the Hebrew children to the Promised Land.

*Then Moses stretched out his hand over the sea, and the
LORD drove the sea back by a strong east wind all night
and made the sea dry land, and the waters were divided.*
EXODUS 14:21 ESV

*And the children of Israel went into the midst of the sea
upon the dry ground: and the waters were a wall unto
them on their right hand, and on their left.*
EXODUS 14:22 KJV

That Scripture should jumpstart your faith if you didn't have any before. If God did that for Moses, just think what He could and would do for you! Not believing that God will show up for us is a trap most of us fall into at some point in our lives. We forget that God is the same yesterday, today, and forever. We forget that He is no respecter of persons. He doesn't just help the mighty or the famous. He helps us all. If we stay grounded and in the Word of God every day and learn to know when the enemy is coming (even before he gets here), we can become stronger and more powerful in fighting against him. Your best may not be here just yet, but it's coming! God has His eyes on you and no matter what the situation, He will always see you through!

No matter where you are at in your walk with God, He has a plan to prosper you and give you life more abundantly. We do not all walk, talk, look, or act the same way, but the Spirit that lives inside us is the same, a Spirit of passion that speaks life into this world, brings light to even the darkest places, speaks healings and strength to the sick and the broken, and make a difference in this world one person at a time. When you look within your heart, what is your passion? What does your soul burn for? Does it burn for God or does it burn for your own wants and needs?

*Now may the God of peace himself sanctify you completely,
and may your whole spirit and soul and body be kept
blameless at the coming of our Lord Jesus Christ.*
I THESSALONIANS 5:23 ESV

For the word of God is living and active, sharper than any two-edged sword, piercing to the division of soul and of spirit, of joints and of marrow, and discerning the thoughts and intentions of the heart.
HEBREWS 4:12 ESV

But I say, walk by the Spirit, and you will not gratify the desires of the flesh. For the desires of the flesh are against the Spirit, and the desires of the Spirit are against the flesh, for these are opposed to each other, to keep you from doing the things you want to do.
GALATIANS 5:16-17 ESV

God loves us. His dream for us is to grow, evolve, and become new creatures for His glory. His glory, not our glory, Amen! He does not want us to stay the same, so he heals our hurts that hold us back and fills us with His goodness. God's Spirit dwells in us from the moment we accept Christ as our Savior. Then the Holy Spirit begins to convict us of things we are doing that are wrong in God's eyes so we know that we need to stop. The Holy Spirit also guides us on the path that God originally had set for our lives. It is never God's fault that we get lost and get sidetracked or go off course, but it is always by our thoughts and actions distract us, and we have to find our back to the road of righteousness. God never leaves us, and we can go back and find Him right where we left him.

But when He, the Spirit of truth, comes, He will guide you into all the truth; for He will not speak on His own initiative, but whatever He hears, He will speak; and He will disclose to you what is to come.
JOHN 16:13 NASB

which things we also speak, not in words taught by human wisdom, but in those taught by the Spirit, combining spiritual thoughts with spiritual words.
I CORINTHIANS 2:13 NASB

For all who are led by the Spirit of God are the sons of God.
ROMANS 8:14 NET BIBLE

*And your ears shall hear a word behind you, saying,
"This is the way, walk in it," when you turn to the right or
when you turn to the left.*
ISAIAH 30:21 ESV

*But the Helper, the Holy Spirit, whom the Father will send
in My name, He will teach you all things, and bring to
your remembrance all that I said to you.*
JOHN 14:26 NASB

Because we were nonbelievers before accepting Jesus Christ as our Lord and Savior, we didn't understand much about the Bible or what it tried to teach us. Normally, it just sat in the same spot for months at a time gathering dust and never opened. When we chose to read it, a new world of possibilities and hope came to live that catapulted our dreams into action.

Some people are still skeptical, and others just laugh at the thought that God created mankind, placed each star in its exact place, and knew exactly what the earth needed to work with the sun and the moon. However, as we go through life and experience things, there comes a time ask ourselves, "Was that God?"

If you have ask yourself that question, you are already saying that you believe in Him, but that you just don't want to live for Him. Life comes easy to some, but the journey is hard for most. The things of this world and the plots and plans of the enemy will hurt you, break you down, cause you to feel that your dreams are unreachable, and make you feel as though your courage has been tossed into the sea never to return. But with God you are found and all that the enemy took from you will be restored!

I am living proof that even though you may not have had the best life as a child, you can achieve double victory in later life when you develop a relationship with Christ. He will move in your past, present, and future to work all things together for good for those who love the Lord and are called according to His purpose (Romans 8:28). He is here to change, mold, and prepare you for the future, a future with His vision in mind. The dream of the first Dreamer (God) is that we all help one another (love your neighbor as yourself, Matthew 22:39) and that we develop ourselves (study to show thyself approved, II Timothy 2:15), and raise up other people to do the same (Romans 10:14) so that we may live for Jesus Christ and proclaim the victory and spread the Gospel and the good news all over the world (Mark 16:15). God saw Earth as a preparation zone for Heaven. We are here to do great and mighty things in the name of Jesus Christ, and to help make a difference in this world.

You turned my wailing into dancing; you removed my sackcloth and clothed me with joy,
PSALM 30:11 NIV

And we know that in all things God works for the good of those who love him, who have been called according to his purpose.
ROMANS 8:28 NIV

"I have told you these things, so that in me you may have peace. In this world you will have trouble. But take heart! I have overcome the world."
JOHN 16:33 NIV

You, dear children, are from God and have overcome them, because the one who is in you is greater than the one who is in the world.
I JOHN 4:4 NIV

Fight the good fight of the faith. Take hold of the eternal life to which you were called when you made your good confession in the presence of many witnesses.
I TIMOTHY 6:12 NIV

God delivered me from many things and healed my heart, soul, and mind. My life as a child was full of misery, fear, anguish, abuse, and many sleepless nights. But when I bowed down to God, put my trust in Him, and asked Him to save me, HE DID! He saved me right away, but the transition to a Christian walk did not happen overnight; it took time, healing, my willingness to give up things that were not pleasing to God, growing as a Christian, and learning His Word. All those baby steps led me to the mature Christian walk I have with God today.

Not by works of righteousness which we have done, but according to his mercy he saved us, by the washing of regeneration, and renewing of the Holy Ghost;
TITUS 3:5 KJV

For by grace are ye saved through faith; and that not of yourselves: it is the gift of God: Not of works, lest any man should boast.
EPHESIANS 2:8-9 KJV

That if thou shalt confess with thy mouth the Lord Jesus, and shalt believe in thine heart that God hath raised him from the dead, thou shalt be saved.
ROMANS 10:9 KJV

No man can come to me, except the Father which hath sent me draw him: and I will raise him up at the last day.
JOHN 6:44 KJV

But the salvation of the righteous is of the LORD: he is their strength in the time of trouble.
PSALM 37:39 KJV

Who is the active voice in your life? Is it God, is it the enemy, or is it you? To walk in total victory and live the dream that God intended for you to live, you need to give your life over to God and allow Him to change you, prepare you, and use you in this world as He originally planned. Always be mindful of who you listen to, who you choose to confide in, and the footsteps you follow, for it might be the very ones that cause you to stumble and fall.

The Out of Place Limb: Bent but Never Broken

We all feel out of place sometimes. However, even if you feel God knows exactly where you are. Ask yourself if you are the type of person who lives in the now, the then, or the future. What are you attached to that you need to let go of and what needs to be your focus to get you to the point of encouraging others? Very often we get too busy thinking about our futures, and we stop being true disciples for Jesus Christ in the present. If we are honest with ourselves, we all fight this daily, and we shouldn't. In every step that we take, we should be in the will of God. We need to focus on the *be* in God's will and then allow the *do* to come. Don't continue hiding in the *doing* of things that take up your time, but start revealing who you are in *being* a true disciple of Jesus Christ in all areas of your life.

> *But seek ye first the kingdom of God, and his*
> *righteousness; and all these things shall be added unto you.*
> MATTHEW 6:33 KJV

With the daily hustle and bustle of life, we unnoticeably leave God out. He needs to be our priority. I have found myself repenting on this subject daily. I do well for a couple of months, and then allow the enemy to creep in and take my focus from *God first* to *life first*. We know not to do this so why do we let it happen? We let it happen because we get side tracked. Pray for the ability to stay focused in all you do. No matter what activities you are involved in, make your walk with God just as important as all the activities you partake in!

That is even important in the church. I don't know how many people get caught up in doing everything they can to show others they are serious about their position in the church and working in the Body of Christ for the Kingdom of God. But many have the wrong heart or do these things for show and for the wrong reasons. We do not want our walk with God to be stunted, lessening our sowing and bringing people to Christ. Pray for balance in your life, and ask The Holy Spirit to help lead the way. We can't just dump the problem on God and expect Him to fix it. We have to do our part and focus every aspect of our lives on His will.

And be not conformed to this world: but be ye transformed by the renewing of your mind, that ye may prove what is that good, and acceptable, and perfect, will of God.
Romans 12:2 KJV

I strive to teach my children to value their lives and to help others do the same, to walk in thankfulness for everything that God has given us, and to give back to the world just as much as God gives to us. I am a single mother of two, a full-time employee, have a son in boy scouts and a daughter in basketball, and have the responsibility of being a full-time student. I am not going to lie, there are times when my life is way too busy worry about other people. But I know God asks more of me. So, I choose to be available even if my current schedule doesn't say that I have time, I make time! The Word of God tells us:

Carry each other's burdens, and in this way you will fulfill the law of Christ.
Galatians 6:2 NIV

It is difficult to set priorities in a busy life. At times, I find myself putting my busy life ahead of God and fellowshipping with His people. When I get crazy busy, I must take time alone, just me and God, and ask Him for strength for myself and others in need. When I reflect on my personal time with God, He has a way of relaxing me and bringing peace to my heart. If you continue to talk with Him and let Him know your struggles and the struggles of others, you can always count on Him bringing assurance and peace over your situations, and the situations of others you are praying for or encouraging. When it comes to being a single mother, He reminds me that I am not alone and that He is always with me. That is also true for you!

The LORD is thy keeper: the LORD is thy shade upon thy right hand. The sun shall not smite thee by day, nor the moon by night. The LORD shall preserve thee from all evil: he shall preserve thy soul. The LORD shall preserve thy going out and thy coming in from this time forth, and even for evermore.
PSALM 121:5-8 KJV

On the job, God reminds us that we are a light for all to see. While you are out working in the world, keep your eyes open and your heart pure to help those that He sends you. I am not going to lie and say this has been easy for me. Sometimes it is hard, and some days I don't even want to go in because of the spiritual warfare it involves. When you work with people who are not living for Christ and who gossip, say the Lord's name in vain, speak negatively, discuss getting drunk, spend their time putting others down, you really don't want to be there. I had to learn that God kept me there for a reason just as He is keeping you there. Maybe you are the only piece of God they get each day. We don't understand, but we are to trust Him and be patient.

We can minister wherever we are. We can be in the grocery store, in a prison, at the movie theatre, or even in the bathroom at Walmart and minister to someone. Always put Him first! It is about Him and not about us, although He is using us to help make a difference in the world. What a great opportunity we have in helping others when we teach them the benefits of putting God first and what it brings to their lives. God reminds us that even though we are busy with our own lives, we are still called to be the light of the world.

"You are the light of the world. A town built on a hill cannot be hidden. Neither do people light a lamp and put it under a bowl. Instead they put it on its stand, and it gives

light to everyone in the house. In the same way, let your light shine before others, that they may see your good deeds and glorify your Father in heaven.
MATTHEW 5:14-16 NIV

When you let your light shine, you give others a sense of hope and freedom. God will help you in every aspect of your life if you allow Him to. Even though we are busy, we can still take a moment and say, "How am I going to put God first in this situation or at this place in my life?" Allow the Holy Spirit to answer you, and then take the necessary steps to do what He tells you to do. Also, keep in mind that it is good to help others and be a light, but you can't do it all. The world may have all kinds of things for you to do, but if it's not God's will for your life, it is okay to say no. Too many times we say yes knowing that we cannot give up any more of our time or that we are actually called to do something different. We need to be honest with ourselves and say no when we are not led by God to say yes. This helps us understand who we are and who Christ is in us! Say no when necessary and walk in Faith.

CHAPTER 9

Turn Your Faith Level into Your Reality Level

And without faith it is impossible to please him,
for whoever would draw near to God must believe that he
exists and that he rewards those who seek him.
HEBREWS 11:6 ESV

Faith without works is dead! Fear is not fun, but it is something we can get past with God's help. God is still working on me with that right now. I always worried about what others thought of me, and I always wanted to please others and make other people happy (because I just like to make other people happy, it brings joy to my heart). Well, by doing this for the wrong reasons, I didn't know that I was taking away from me and my opinions, thoughts, feelings, and say so. Too much YES and not enough No.

I fear speaking in front of big crowds. I plan to evangelize and become a motivational speaker at some point, so God expects me to get over my fear to do all that He has called me to do. You know that feeling you get when you are in front of an audience, and everything that you knew and planned to say is quickly wiped away from your memory? That is the fear and anxiety I am talking about. We must face and get over our fears, whatever they are. We must RISE and do the things that we don't necessarily feel comfortable doing.

There will be times of hardship and pain, but if we choose to RISE TO THE MISSION, then we know God will help us through.

Knock, Knock.

Who's there?

Today's challenge is at your door.

What are you going to do? You will either allow it to overtake you or you will rise above it and conquer! You may feel afraid at first, but you do not have to continue walking in fear. The enemy tries to use fear against us, but we know deep in our hearts that we have the Holy Spirit helping us. The Holy Spirit comforts us; He speaks courage and strength over us, He gives us every opportunity to search for Him and stand in His presence with thanksgiving and a peace of mind no matter what comes our way. Each time I speak, before I say a word, I ask the Holy Spirit to come before me and give me the courage and the words to speak into the hearts of the souls that are listening. It works every time. Have you started walking in lazy holiness due to life situations or are you someone who decides to be active in the Spirit of the Lord and move when God says move? Do you trust Him when He tells you that He will fight your battles and you need not be afraid? (II Chronicles 20:17).

I once was passive, but now I have chosen to move when God tells me to go. I have turned into an assertive Christian that remains respectful to the belief of others. I try to move only when God tells me to. A lot of Christians move before asking God in prayer to show them what to do. Sometimes doors are opened, but are they the right opportunities? We must take prayer and God's voice seriously as we move forward. We are at the end times brothers and sisters, and we don't have time to mess around. We cannot continue to put our ideas, decisions, and feelings ahead of God. We walk because of Him. We talk because of Him. We will live eternally because of Him. He has done and continues to do many things for us, but what are you doing for Him?

The Lord is my shepherd; I shall not want.
PSALM 23:1 KJV

God will instruct me and teach me in the way I should go. He will guide me with His eye (Psalm 32:8). My steps are ordered by the Lord (Psalm 37:23). His Word is a lamp to my feet and a light to my path

(Psalm 119:105). I trust in the Lord with all my heart and lean not on my own understanding. In all my ways, I acknowledge Him and he directs my path (Proverbs 3:5-6). I desire to do God's will so I shall know whether it is from God (John 7:17). I will stand perfect and complete in all the will of God (Colossians 4:12).

Whether or not we are in denial, Jesus is coming soon! Don't force your beliefs on others because God gives us all free will, but encourage them, and those that want to change will listen. There are still moments that I don't speak up when I need to because of fear, not always knowing what to say about God, or because I am at work among nonbelievers, but sometimes God just says, "Don't say anything. Just remain silent." Silence is not a sign of weakness. It just means that a wise person knows when to speak and when to listen. The enemy can bend us, but He can't break us unless we allow Him to.

Sometimes silence is key! Choose to observe and then speak truth. Also, don't continue to be silent in fear because of not wanting others to judge you. Be wise. Deal with the issues, let them go, and give them to God. You no longer need to live in continual fear of yourself or others, not on God's watch.

God never said that we wouldn't have obstacles, but that we would be able to stand in confidence and with power. We still have a lot of growing up to do. None of us have hit the stopping point of growing. We are never too mature to grow, Amen! Learn how to listen to others that have "been there and done that." Use others' experiences and wise counsel to speed up your journey. Don't allow pride to hold you back from the future possibilities. I say possibilities because if you are not where you need to be to receive them, then they could go to someone else who has earned them.

You will be enriched in every way so that you can
be generous on every occasion, and through us your
generosity will result in thanksgiving to God.
This service that you perform is not only supplying the
needs of the Lord's people but is also overflowing
in many expressions of thanks to God.
II CORINTHIANS 9:11-12 NIV

There will be days of happiness and days of sadness, days of laughs and days of tears. Days of strength and days of weakness, but in Him, we will find the strength needed. We can now have peace over any situation because of the love and power of Jesus Christ. By reading His truth, I know that He will provide me with whatever I may need, despite what is going on in my life. If I need healing, He will be my healer. If I need protection, He will be my protector. If I need financial help, He will be my provider.

He gives power to the weak and strength to the powerless.
ISAIAH 40:29 NLT

It is my job to find His truth and place it in my heart to keep it forever. There is light at the end of your tunnel and a rainbow after your rainy day. We already have the victory, so now is the time to claim it in Jesus Name! The power inspired by the divine Spirit will give you the endurance you need at the time you need it. Did you know that you had the victory even before you were born?! Yes, I know. Hard to believe, right? Well, not really. Jesus came to die for your sins so that you could be set free. He took the death for YOU! He paid the ultimate price so that you could live in abundance and have eternal life.

But thanks be to God! He gives us the victory
through our Lord Jesus Christ.
I CORINTHIANS 15:57 NIV

When you fight the enemy, what is your normal weapon of defense? It should be the Word of God, which is truth and constant. It never changes. God's Word stays true and remains within your heart and works deep within your soul. Why? To bring others to Christ and to keep you focused. Your testimony is just what someone else needs to hear. Your brokenness will help bring freedom to another individual through the power of Jesus Christ! There will be storms along the way, but you will have peace from beginning to end. It may start out rocky, but it will end on a smooth surface.

The waters are hid as with a stone,
and the face of the deep is frozen.
JOB 38:30 KJV

Capture this moment! Are you currently living in faith or in fear? Who says you can't do it?! Your coworkers on the job, your family, your so-called friends, your neighbor down the street, or maybe even the kids at school … I have some good news! Your future is not in their hands but in God's hands. You are now connected to someone whose opinion matters more than anyone else's here on earth. When others put you down and say that you are not good enough or that the dream that you see in your future isn't for you, God says you CAN! Too many times we allow our dreams, goals, and ambitions to be put on the back burner while the things of this world come first. What in the world are we thinking? Why would we give attention to the things that keep us from our destiny? Why spend countless hours of our time and energy doing what the enemy wants us to do? It is because we get caught up in the past. Past sins and past failures are the worst, especially when others bring them up, but you need to say, "NO!" Don't be scared to tell your testimony (your real testimony). God already forgave you so what others bring up is not for you any longer. Move along!

The LORD is on my side; I will not fear:
what can man do unto me?
PSALM 118:6 KJV

Be an example of God's mercy and grace. I am not ashamed of my past like I once was. I have freedom in Jesus Christ and you will too. You can't change the past, but you can reshape your future into whatever God has ordained it to be. You are wiser, and now you are protected in the wings of His angels. The more you follow His voice, the closer you get to Jesus, and the stronger you become. You will never go back to those dead things that you used to do and the things you once were. God has broken those chains that kept you in bondage all this time and has freed you in Jesus Name, and we say, Amen!

God is in control, but we need to step up, not back up! It is time to take charge of your life and give that devil a big kick in the booty! How? Well, here we go! Start by making a list and separate the things in our lives into God's corner and enemy's corner. Sometimes we need to see things on paper to better understand and put them in perspective, (also it allows us to speak it into the atmosphere). Next, we get rid of anything that is not in God's corner! No more excuses. Make room for the things in God's corner and watch your life start changing for the better. Focus on the things that will make a difference in your life and bring you closer to God.

> *All things are lawful for me, but not all things*
> *are profitable. All things are lawful for me,*
> *but I will not be mastered by anything.*
> I CORINTHIANS 6:12 NASB

Remember, God will give you the necessary tools and resources to do what He has put in your heart; He just asks that you seek Him first. Also, keep His Word in your heart, pray with power, and keep looking forward. You will then realize that *I'm not able to do this* turns into *God, I couldn't have done that without you.* He will sustain you! There are endless treasures when Jesus comes first in your life and situations. He is the center of a solid foundation, and He always keeps His promises! On your mark, get set, GO: Start believing that God can and that He WILL!

The In and Out Believer

Faith is powerful, but it is for the hot Christian, not the cold or lukewarm Christian. "In and Out" believers will not live the life that God has intended. So, if you are an in and out believer, stop blaming God and others for your relationship not being as close as it should be. We react to situations and often behave in ways that do not complement who we are as individuals and that are in conflict with our faith levels.

Many think that our behavior should depend on the situation, but if you are a child of God, no matter the situation you are to act like a child of God. Claim your freedom! It has already been given to you. Believe it, Receive it, and Step into it! Your walk will produce change! Be ready! God has something in store for you on the other side of that mountain you are climbing. Build your character carefully and with much thought so that God can use you for more than He can use you now. When you strengthen yourself, your mind, and your knowledge, God will elevate you to the next level. Start living each day to please God. Pray with faith, pray with power, and ask for bigger than what you need. Too many people ask for small, so they receive small. If we ask for bigger (because our God is bigger), He will give us what we ask, in His time, of course.

> *Delight yourself in the Lord, and he will give you the desires of your heart.*
> PSALM 37:4 ESV

Just to show you how having faith in a situation works with prayer, I will share with you a time in my life when I really needed faith to receive. I had to have a tremendous amount of faith to believe that God would break alcoholism in certain members of my family. I prayed and prayed for people in my family to quit drinking, fighting, and mentally abusing themselves and others. After years of praying, they quit drinking! Thank you, Jesus! God answered those prayers of mine because of my faith and obedience, but also because He has a plan for their lives as well! After we are saved and know God's promises, we must stand in the gap for our family members and friends. The Word of God says that He will save you and those around you.

> *Take heed unto thyself, and unto the doctrine; continue in them: for in doing this thou shalt both save thyself, and them that hear thee.*
> I TIMOTHY 4:16 KJV

Since some of my family members have quit drinking, things have been better for them, and for those around them. They might not know the goodness of the Lord in fullness, but in time, God will reveal Himself. I will never give up on my family. I will continue to pray until the day I take my last breath. My faith remains in God and His Word. God's timing is not always our timing. Some journeys just take longer than others, so we need to pray for ourselves, our families, and for peace in this world and direction for our leaders!

> *For to set the mind on the flesh is death, but to set the mind on the Spirit is life and peace.*
> ROMANS 8:6 ESV

It is easy for me to rest at night because I am at peace with God, but many others in this world do not have peace. You may be one of them. God wants us to have peace. No matter what the day has brought upon you, the sadness that you may feel, or the sin that you may have committed, give it to God and allow Him to cover you and surround you with peace and comfort that sustains you till morning. Then, you will begin another day with new mercies and new adventures in Him.

> *For his anger is but for a moment, and his favor is for a lifetime. Weeping may tarry for the night, but joy comes with the morning.*
> PSALM 30:5 ESV

We are born with treasure and gifts within us to be used specifically for our divine purpose. With faith and peace, we can begin our journey. God provides us with a road to take, directions to get where He wants us to go, and gives us endurance for the journey. Jesus has walked the sands of the desert and has traveled along the bluest of waters. He knows exactly what is ahead of us. Therefore, God gives us tools and resources needed to accomplish our mission while on this earth.

*Now to each one the manifestation of the Spirit
is given for the common good.*
I Corinthians 12:7 NIV

*For to one is given through the Spirit the utterance
of wisdom, and to another the utterance of knowledge
according to the same Spirit, to another faith by the same
Spirit, to another gifts of healing by the one Spirit,
to another the working of miracles, to another prophecy,
to another the ability to distinguish between spirits,
to another various kinds of tongues, to another the
interpretation of tongues. All these are empowered
by one and the same Spirit, who apportions
to each one individually as he wills.*
I Corinthians 12:8-11 ESV

Ever notice that we listen to others about our giftings and do what we think we should do, only to discover that God has different plans? We have to consult Him first! It is important that we discovery our gifts and then magnify them. Pray for God to show you what to do in order to magnify these gifts. Prayer works and allows God to reveal things to you that you would not know without that close, personal relationship with Him. He wants to talk with you just as a parent wants to talk with and to their children. He wants to know that you care about His will for your life and that your number one priority is Him, and that you trust His decisions and plans for your life.

*But seek ye first the kingdom of God, and his
righteousness; and all these things shall be added unto you.*
Matthew 6:33 KJV

I recall one evening at service asking God to help me with my debts. I thanked Him in advance. I knew it was asking a lot in the natural, but I knew God was supernatural and owned the cattle on a thousand hills. My debts were nothing to him, not even a drop in the bucket.

He could do it. I had faith in Him. I prayed that He would continue taking care of us, but that He would make my debt less so that I could provide better for my family. Because my faith level was my reality level, God blessed my children and me. God told me to put a hundred-dollar bill into offering that day, which was more than what I normally did or could afford. Because God said it, I did it. As soon as I put that money into offering, I opened heaven so that He could pour out His blessings on me! Two days later, I went to make a car payment on a car that still had ten thousand dollars left to pay off. They said they would send me a letter in the mail stating that it was taken care of and that I no longer had to pay that debt. I started literally jumping up and down, and tears started flowing down my cheeks. I knew that it was God! It was the timing. I made sure to thank Him for that. God blesses many who never say, "Thank you." We must continue to thank Him in the bad times as well as the good times because it could always be worse. Never stop thanking God, never stop putting in your tithes, and never stop praying because He hears you. He will always give you what you need. It may not be when you want it (God likes to wait sometimes until the last possible second so that you know it is Him who showed up to save the day), but continue in faith, and He will provide.

Be brave in your walk with God. Have the courage like an eagle, and the honor of a dove. Be determined in all you do because the Lord orders your steps. With all you do, remember to be humble and to love. Be grateful and lend a helping hand any time you can. Nothing happens by chance. If God places something on your heart, pray about it. If God places someone in your life, ask God if he or she is from Him. Have faith in your questions and prayers, and He will confirm the answers through the breath of resurrection.

For I, saith the LORD, will be unto her a wall of fire round about, and will be the glory in the midst of her.
ZECHARIAH 2:5 KJV

CHAPTER 10

The Breath of Resurrection

*"Truly, truly, I say to you, he who hears My word,
and believes Him who sent Me, has eternal life, and does
not come into judgment, but has passed out of death into
life. "Truly, truly, I say to you, an hour is coming and now
is, when the dead will hear the voice of the Son of God,
and those who hear will live.*
JOHN 5:24-25 NASB

We grow up hearing, "You can be anything you want to be." After much thought on this, I have concluded that we can only be what we want to be if we are led in the right direction. This first begins with how we grow up and what we are taught. It is sad to see a young child who has talent, but has parents who will not support the child's dreams. Believing or not believing in a child can have a major impact on their lives both today and in the future. I know it affected me. I was lucky and had a mother that was just as good at softball as I was. I believe I got my talent from her, but my family is full of softball players. When she realized how good I was, she put everything she had into helping me succeed as a player. She even became a bus driver and went to most of the games with me. She was my biggest fan, and coached me as a child until I got into high school.

Without her support and time, I probably would not have become one of the best catchers in Southeast Missouri. I received awards and trophies, All-District, All-Conference, and All-Tournament recognition.

But, even though I was good enough, my mother's investment of time and encouragement helped me to get farther than I would have without her help. You see, it is our job to breathe life into others as God breathes life into us. It will take our time and effort to help others succeed. You know that you can be anything that you want to be, and you have to encourage and develop that confidence in others as well. Regardless of your past, or even your present reality, if you have the right people in your life, sent by God to lift you up, you will be successful.

I have always been someone who likes to stay on the side lines and watch others succeed, but God has started raising me up. I always encourage others, I support others as my mother showed me how, and I respect others because I want to be respected in return. God's vision is our mission. He wants us to push others to be better and to grow. He wants us to take time out of our days to encourage others. He wants us to love others and show them what true love is, and He wants His Word to be life to those that need fresh air! His breathe is our resurrection tool.

Be an instrument in the Body of Christ and carry out your mission. God has entrusted us as His chosen vessels to hold His treasure deep within, and share it piece by piece with those in this world. Your life will be turned upside down before you enter His will. The worldly things inside you that are at enmity with God must die before your resurrection can begin.

> *But some man will say, How are the dead raised up? and*
> *with what body do they come? Thou fool, that which thou*
> *sowest is not quickened, except it die: And that which thou*
> *sowest, thou sowest not that body that shall be, but bare*
> *grain, it may chance of wheat, or of some other grain:*
> *But God giveth it a body as it hath pleased him,*
> *and to every seed his own body.*
> I CORINTHIANS 15: 35-38 KJV

Always walk with the Lord in front of you. Never take the glory of God away from Him and put it upon yourself. Even as a catcher, I always knew that God gave me my talent. He could have just as easily taken it away and given it to someone else, but He chose to allow me to experience the joy of being a competitive athlete.

Not unto us, O LORD, not unto us, but unto thy name
give glory, for thy mercy, and for thy truth›s sake.
Psalm 115:1 KJV

Leave this world better than you found it! Follow your internal drive. You will never know who or what will benefit from it. Don't rush your life away, but cherish every moment that you are still alive. God is not finished with you! No more taking things for granted. We get so busy that we forget just to breathe and live in the moment. God does not want you to worry about anything; He just asks that you live for Him and let Him direct your path.

Take therefore no thought for the morrow: for the morrow
shall take thought for the things of itself. Sufficient unto
the day is the evil thereof.
Matthew 6:34 KJV

Uncomfortable moments empower you for the future. We should want Jesus to have the same testimony for us that we have for ourselves. Continue the road to finding who you are and what God wants you to do each day, continue to claim the freedom in which God has already given you, and continue taking steps closer to your destiny. We need to focus on restoration, expansion, and prosperity for the world in which we live.

There is an old you, then there is a new you, but the one I love the most is the God in us! You will always be the sparrow, and God will always continue to watch over you. We may not die with a lot of things, but we will die with Jesus, Amen! With Him, you will never go without.

Reach for the high call of God. Be mighty in the Body of Christ and lead the way so that others can follow. God has proven to be trustworthy, dependable, loving, honest, respectful, courteous, merciful, and of good character. He has placed these same qualities and attributes in us. Choose to live for Jesus, and not die in the hand of the enemy.

From Death to Resurrection, I owe it to God, the original Dreamer. The dream may be shaken in some right now, but they will never be broken in the gates of forgiveness. Hidden deep within our hearts lies passion and destiny just waiting for us to step into. Passion that will manifest after the trials and tribulations of our actions and life's most valuable lessons. From the suffering and the tears, we bring forth smiles and get rid of those fears. We were created to carry out the dream, the Dreamer's Dream, the first and the last, the maker and the taker of life and the strength of our tomorrows. The thoughts, actions, and words of our Redeemer provide us with favor. The vision of yesterday will soon develop the mission for tomorrow. The fall of our past is what is now allowing us to walk in victory. In our falling, we rose, and now that we have risen, it is time to carry out His vision. We are on a mission, and now this is our season! Our time to RISE UP and be all that God has intended us to be. With His love, you will do great things; your light will shine and beam among many, for the dreamer in you is ready to be unleashed and made new. The dream will be forever reachable as long as you keep your heart teachable. You're a diamond among the hundreds of stones, so stand up and be the dream of the original dreamer, for in abundance new life will appear. Then you will know Jesus is near!

Guard, through the Holy Spirit who dwells in us,
the treasure which has been entrusted to you.
II TIMOTHY 1:14 NASB

But the fruit of the Spirit is love, joy, peace, longsuffering,
gentleness, goodness, faith, Meekness, temperance:
against such there is no law.
GALATIANS 5:22-23 KJV

But the anointing that you received from him abides in
you, and you have no need that anyone should teach you.
But as his anointing teaches you about everything, and is
true, and is no lie — just as it has taught you, abide in him.
I JOHN 2:27 ESV

I Once Was Blind, But Now I See

I once was blind, but now I see, Yay me! I didn't see the whole picture before I gave my life to Christ, but now I see things from a different perspective. We have to work together and come together with one accord to make a difference. There was a time I could not see that I needed to step out and come forth, but God revealed it to me. He has resurrected my mind and illuminated my soul. Now I live each day loving others and doing more for them than what I do for myself. My children will have a future filled with God because I care about their futures and the futures of the children to come. Whenever I go home to be with the Lord, I want to make sure I leave my children and grandchildren with Jesus and with the capacity to love others and the desire to do more for others than they do for themselves. I am going to start a vision board with them to get them prepared to take steps to achieve their goals, and I encourage you to do the same. My friend Nina and I were discussing making a vision board, and I thought it was a perfect idea for the kids as well. If you don't have kids, then make a vision board for yourself. I remember making one when I was in high school. I wrote down a car, diploma, apartment, softball scholarship, and a job. I achieved every single one of them because I wrote them down and placed them on my wall so that I could see them every day. When you see something that you want every day, it makes you want it that much more.

> *Look not every man on his own things, but every man also on the things of others. Let this mind be in you, which was also in Christ Jesus: Who, being in the form of God, thought it not robbery to be equal with God: But made himself of no reputation, and took upon him the form of a servant, and was made in the likeness of men:*
> PHILIPPIANS 2:4-7 KJV

I took steps to achieve my goals and you can, too. It's time to bring unity back, and to finish what we started, but quit doing! One person can't help everyone. There are people in this world that I am not able to help. There are people in this world that you will not be able to help, but somebody else that has gone through or is going through the same thing can help. Help someone get where they are going, and God will help you get where He wants you to be.

> s each has received a gift, use it to serve one another,
> as good stewards of God's varied grace:
> I PETER 4:10 ESV

Don't point your finger at others, but instead consider looking in a mirror and evaluating yourself. To work with our brothers and sisters, we need to have the right spirit and be led with the heart of God. It is the sides of the mountain that sustains life, not the tip. So focus on the journey. Even people you think have it all together sometimes don't. We all go through seasons. Choose not to judge others, but to love them despite your differences. Appreciate those that make you laugh and those that make you cry because there is always a reason for the happiness and sadness in our lives, and always a new lesson learned. We learn from one another from the good as well as the bad. This is where we need wise counsel. They have been there and done that, Amen! Stay true to yourself, men and women of God. You would much rather try and fail than to not try at all. Eventually, that failure can become another victory, another sin in return for a WIN! Always choose to be the bigger person. Be a positive role model for others so that others can see you for who you truly are and want to unite together.

> for he was a good man, full of the Holy Spirit and of faith.
> And large numbers of people were added to the Lord.
> ACTS 11:24 HOLMAN CHRISTIAN STANDARD BIBLE

Stretch yourself and others to the point of no limitation, no fear, and no excuses. Push harder to be stronger mentally, physically, and spiritually in the Lord. Be like a tree floating in the wind. No matter how hard the wind blows, it still can't knock down the tree. Life happens, people hurt you, there are disappointments, delays, and things we have no control over. Still be like the tree and just stay planted in the Word of God, stay strong in your faith, and keep holding onto His promises. This is your race under His terms, so pace yourself wisely. It's because of Jesus that we will never be the same!

Be of good courage, and he shall strengthen your heart,
all ye that hope in the LORD.
PSALM 31:24 KJV

God gives every person in the world a purpose. We should all be treated with dignity, respect, and love no matter our race, religion, or background. Your ability to communicate with God reflects that you are made in His image. He created and approves of us all, so racism needs to end. We are more worried about the color of someone's skin than fixing the actual problems within ourselves. We are all loved, not worthless; we are all needed, not disregarded.

So Peter opened his mouth and said: "Truly I understand
that God shows no partiality, but in every nation anyone
who fears him and does what is right is acceptable to him.
ACTS 10:34-35 ESV

We are the example! Just because someone is different does not mean that or she is better, it just means that God made us differently to reach people in ways that only we can reach them. You are made for a unique reason and so are your brothers and sisters, so let us Rise to the Mission. United we stand together; but divided we fall, crumble, and separate!

God gives us 20/20 vision even in the wilderness. In *The Life You've Always Wanted: Spiritual Disciplines for Ordinary People*, John Ortberg said, "Sometimes we must live with the "latch off the door." Sometimes we need to be available to talk or pray with troubled people - people whom we will not be able to "cure" and who can't contribute to our career success." (Zondervan, 2009). Thy will be done in Jesus' name! Don't you dare fear the unknown! God gives us vision and direction. Don't allow the tactics of the enemy keep you from advancing in the Kingdom of

God. Satan has already lost the battle, Amen! Jesus is coming back, and isn't it nice to know that this is not our home but merely a preparation shelter for what is to come?

It is important to know the process of walking in God's Word: First we share our testimonies and speak the Gospel. That helps God convert people to Christ (but although God uses us as His vessel, He does not need us. If we did not speak for God, even the rocks would cry out (Luke 19:40). When new converts become disciples just like we did, they learn to work and serve in the body of Christ. As they grow, God produces leaders and forms a powerful unity of believers.

In Revelation, John says,

> *And I heard a great voice out of heaven saying, Behold,*
> *the tabernacle of God is with men, and he will dwell with*
> *them, and they shall be his people, and God himself shall*
> *be with them, and be their God. And God shall wipe away*
> *all tears from their eyes; and there shall be no more death,*
> *neither sorrow, nor crying, neither shall there be any more*
> *pain: for the former things are passed away.*
> REVELATION 21: 3-4 KJV

That is great news for the people of God! That is what we look forward to. Hallelujah! We are now standing on the training ground but already have the victory. Be on fire for God; let His Word burn inward, forward, and through your soul. You will continue to face hard tribulations at times, but it is not darkness anymore, it is but light that goes dim on the outside of you but still shines brightly on the inside of you. Allow your light to radiate through even during hard times. Unleash His power from within!

In *The Annotated Hobbit: The Hobbit, Or, There and Back Again (Middle-Earth Universe)*, J.R.R. Tolkien said, "May the wind under your wings bear you not where the sun sails and the moon walks" (Houghton Mifflin, 1990). I absolutely love this and will always hold it dear. Hope it touches your heart as well and helps you as it has helped me. Another one that has always stayed with me that I pray that helps you in the same regard.

Ibrahim Emile is famous for saying, "Believers do not carry their faith; faith is their wings. They will soar on wings like eagles; they will run and not grow weary." The Scripture states in Isaiah 40:31:

> *But they that wait upon the Lord shall renew*
> *their strength; they shall mount up with wings*
> *as eagles; they shall run, and not be weary;*
> *and they shall walk, and not faint.*
> KJV

In *Conformed to His Image*, Kenneth D. Boa once said, "We teach what we believe, but we reproduce what we are" (Harper Collins, 2009). This is one of the most powerful revelations that we could ever realize. How many times do you truly believe something that you say, but it does not show in your life or your actions? When we walk in the wilderness, we need to be careful about what we say and what we do. If we do not live what we are speaking, then it is best not to say anything at all. If you do, and others see that we live lives of lies, and our actions will produce more people with lives full of lies and deceit. It is important in your walk to truly discover who you are, change, and live a new life as a new creature in Christ. Talk the talk, but walk the walk.

> *Beware of false prophets, which come to you in sheep's*
> *clothing, but inwardly they are ravening wolves. Ye shall*
> *know them by their fruits. Do men gather grapes of thorns,*
> *or figs of thistles? Even so every good tree bringeth forth*
> *good fruit; but a corrupt tree bringeth forth evil fruit.*
> *A good tree cannot bring forth evil fruit, neither can a*
> *corrupt tree bring forth good fruit.*
> MATTHEW 7:15-18 KJV

Just tap into the power of Resurrection, and watch God do amazing things in your life. Today you may be a liar, but tomorrow you can be someone that others trust. We are told to use His power here on earth and not just wait until we get to heaven. Choose to have a relationship with Him, and not have a relationship with religion. Pray that you can see what He sees so that He can use you each day. Always remember to die to yourself daily and repent of your sins because even though we may be living according to His Word now, there could always be a slip up.

Nothing is impossible with God, so start believing it. Without your faith, you have nothing! Peace, love, and joy go hand in hand with resurrection. We have the peace of God that comforts us when we are afraid. Therefore we can rise up and have no fear. The love of God can never be broken, which causes us to Rise for others even when they don't rise for themselves. The comes joy and hope. When there is joy in your heart and hope in your future, you are smiling. Others can see and feel the joy that you carry, and it shines brightly to many. When you allow peace, love, joy, and hope to shine through you every day for others, they will want what you have. They will want to know this God so He can give them the same power to breathe resurrection into their own lives and even the lives of others. Don't wait until the last minute and be forced to suffer because you ran out of time.

CHAPTER 11

Don't Leave with Unfinished Business

Now finish the work, so that your eager willingness
to do it may be matched by your completion of it,
according to your means.
II CORINTHIANS 8:11 NIV

I tell myself every day, "Don't leave here with unfinished business." It is my duty to carry out all that is asked of me. If I would not have Risen above my circumstances and wrote this book, just think of all the people out there that would not get the encouragement that God has hand-picked for them to receive at this very moment. Sometimes things come at just the right time. God is always an on-time God, and even with all the things I was going through while writing this book, I know God will allow it help someone. The enemy starts attacking you harder than ever when you are doing something big in the Kingdom of God. He doesn't like it when another soul is added in the Body of Christ. Know that when you Rise, the enemy will come after you with a vengeance, so be prepared. Do what you have been called to do. You never know who or how many you will help!

Ask God to light a fire in your soul and provide a pathway for your feet, to touch you and open your eyes to understanding. Ask God to pour His knowledge and wisdom into you but also give you revelation deeper and stronger than ever before. Completely surrender your will to God's will from this day forward and seek His help and guidance in all areas of your life. For all your broken pieces that God puts back together, He can use them to fix the broken pieces in someone else because of your testimony. You are the glue sent from God to help the souls in this world come back together and form the core of God again! Say, "Jesus, lead the way, and I shall follow." You were once a small building, but God has made you an empire. He WILL form the empire in you! Manifestation is coming!

Reverend Gilbert M. Beenken once said, "Other men see only a hopeless end, but the Christian rejoices in an endless hope." The sky is the limit when your chains are broken and your freedom is found in Jesus Christ.

> *We are troubled on every side, yet not distressed; we are perplexed, but not in despair; Persecuted, but not forsaken; cast down, but not destroyed; Always bearing about in the body the dying of the Lord Jesus, that the life also of Jesus might be made manifest in our body.*
> II Corinthians 4:8-10 KJV

Our past no longer defines us, but instead a new version of our future selves. We are ever-changing, but that is the beauty of it. Even though our past self is not our present self, our future self is not going to be our present self either. We cannot change our past or the past of others, but we can change how we view ourselves now and who we want to be in the future. Every decision that we make now affects our future in some way. Therefore, it is important to ask God before you make important decisions. Do not make decisions based on emotion because that never helps. I have never known of a good ending when emotions ruled, but if we seek God's answers before taking it upon ourselves to do as we please, then we will continue to stay in God's will, and we will forever remain under His wing.

> *Call unto me, and I will answer thee, and shew thee great and mighty things, which thou knowest not.*
> Jeremiah 33:3 KJV

We do not want to walk down a path of our will because it is easier for the enemy to attack us and break us down if we are not in God's perfect will. We need to continue to read and meditate on His Holy Word daily and continue to have faith in God to stay on our path and fully make the right decisions. We will not get to our future selves on our time, but only on God's time ,which is the perfect time, Amen! There will be road blocks, traffic jams, and missed turns ahead, but we must always stay connected to Jesus and to His spirit which wraps itself like roots to a tree around our hearts!

Fully submit to God and give Him your ears to hear, your heart to love, your soul to keep, your hands to work in the lives of others, your feet to follow in the path of righteousness, and your mind to conform into Himself. Ignite His light within you! It is time to step up and step out! An eagle represents power, freedom, and transcendence. It's time to fly by the open seas just as the beautiful eagle you are!

Behold, I send you forth as sheep in the midst of wolves:
be ye therefore wise as serpents, and harmless as doves.
MATTHEW 10:16 KJV

We all know to be obedient so that we can experience the manifestation. Your voice matters! Your testimony matters! So, get out there and speak life into the lives of others. We say we want change, but never get up to do anything about it. Be the difference that makes the difference. Change you…change the world! Rise Up and raise up leaders who will fear God and seek truth!

Moreover thou shalt provide out of all the people able men,
such as fear God, men of truth, hating covetousness;
and place such over them, to be rulers of thousands,
and rulers of hundreds, rulers of fifties, and rulers of tens:
EXODUS 18:21 KJV

For if a man cannot manage his own household,
how can he take care of God's church?
I TIMOTHY 3:5 NLT

Never give up on others even when going through a tough process. It is not going to be easy, and sometimes we may feel like we do not have the strength, but we must put our feelings aside and help people Rise to the Mission! Sometimes we rise on our own with God's strength and other times God places people in our lives to help develop, strengthen, encourage, and bring us up to where we need to be. Jesus also had a hard time walking in this world which is why He understands us. He succeeded, but He only succeeded because He had the best leader that anyone could ever have. He had God, His Father. He had the Word in His heart and walked in a teachable and proclaiming spirit. He had joy in His heart no matter what the circumstances were for Himself or others.

> *Consider it pure joy, my brothers and sisters,*
> *whenever you face trials of many kinds, because you know*
> *that the testing of your faith produces perseverance.*
> *Let perseverance finish its work so that you may be mature*
> *and complete, not lacking anything.*
> JAMES 1:2-4 NIV

Walk with perseverance, walk with determination, walk with confidence, and teach others to do the same. You learn as you go, others learn as they follow, and some learn as they lead. It is a blessing to be able to learn from God and teach others what He has revealed to you. We must first learn how to follow so that we may grow to lead! Learn today; lead tomorrow. We are training for reigning, Amen! What good is the tree of life in our lives if we are not also gaining and forming revelation?! Wisdom and knowledge are important and needed, but revelation must come after. Then when you gain revelation, you need to mentor someone else. You need to lead others so that they may know the truth also. Rise to the Mission of taking someone by the hand and lifting them up.

> *But he answered, "It is written, "'Man shall not live*
> *by bread alone, but by every word that comes*
> *from the mouth of God.'"*
> MATTHEW 4:4 ESV

Teach those you mentor the right way to live by speaking the Word of God. Raise up people with purpose. There is no greater harm to know that someone is living wrong and was taught wrong, and you knowing the truth, continue to allow them to live that way and walk in defeat without letting them know what you have been taught. The enemy already defeats them. They were defeated as soon as lies were put in their heads. It is our job to Rise Up and open up our mouths and speak truth. It is our job to Rise Up and provide a solid foundation for those that are coming after us. It is our job to Rise Up and contribute and finish what Jesus started!

The Spirit of the Lord is upon me, because he hath anointed me to preach the gospel to the poor; he hath sent me to heal the brokenhearted, to preach deliverance to the captives, and recovering of sight to the blind, to set at liberty them that are bruised, To preach the acceptable year of the Lord.
LUKE 4:18-19 KJV

For the Son of man is come to seek and to save that which was lost.
LUKE 19:10 KJV

Our Mission is to help Jesus in whatever way He asks. Whether you become a teacher, pastor, coach, or parent, do it in love and passion, and with the intention of bringing others into the Body of Christ. Help Jesus save the lost and heal the sick. Help bring happiness to those that are hurting, and peace to those who live in fear.

Your Reward is Worth the Wait

My brother is very important to me, and no matter what he does or doesn't do, I will always love him and be there for him. He is four years younger than me so I pretty much helped take care of him when we were younger. We had to grow up faster than most, and we did it together, so I think of him not only as my brother but as someone who I truly want to do well and flourish in life like a parent would want for their child. I remember the day that my brother got saved, baptized, and filled with the Holy Ghost with evidence of speaking in tongues. It was the best day of my life, other than the birth of my children. I can't begin to describe how thankful I was or the inspiration that came forth afterwards.

On July 31, 2015, I cried out to God, "Please restore my family! Please help my brother search you and find you somehow." I had been praying for a long time for my brother to just get a taste of Christ and His love for him. It was a Friday night when we were having a Section 5 Rally with a guest speaker, and I got this feeling inside of me like God was telling me that tonight was the night. I couldn't help but stop at the house after church and ask him to come to our night service, even though all the other times he said "No."

This time he said, "Yes!" I prayed the rest of that day that he would not change his mind, but we cannot control God's timing. Luckily, when I get to the house to pick him up, he was ready to go. I thought, "Oh yes, Lord. What are you going to do tonight?" We walked into the church and sat down. He was very uncomfortable but sat down with me anyway.

I was attending West Point Pentecostal Church in Doniphan, Missouri, before finding my way to Mt. Calvary Powerhouse Church in Poplar Bluff, Missouri. God places you in different churches for different seasons, and I am thankful for both places. Each one holds a piece of me, and I hold a piece of it.

Worship music came on, I stood up and worshipped, as he sat there and listened. When the preacher got up to preach the Word of God, I recall seeing him roll his eyes a couple of times. I say this because we see this type of thing all the time in church, but even though we see it, we never know what God is about to do. That was just the enemy trying to distract my brother's mind so that he wouldn't receive the Word. BUT GOD brought him in for a reason! If God has a plan, no demon in hell can stop it from happening!

During the altar call. I saw tears in my brother's eyes. My friend Serra, a mighty woman of God, came over to us and she prayed with him. I was very thankful for this moment because sometimes God uses others to do things that you can't do. Even though he was my brother,

God told Serra to walk over and pray for him. I watched as he got up with her and went to the front. I followed. As others and I prayed for him, my brother accepted Jesus Christ into his life. I couldn't believe it! God answered my prayers that I had been praying for such a long time. Never give up on your family because God is always listening.

After he accepted Jesus Christ as his Lord and Savior, Serra asked him if he wanted to be baptized in Jesus Name for the remission of his sins as the Bible tells us to do, and he said, "Yes." As he walked up the steps to redemption, his heart was pounding; my heart was pounding, Serra's heart was pounding (because she knew the feeling of watching your sibling come to Christ and get baptized). We get excited about anyone who finds Jesus, but when it's your sibling, it is even more special.

My brother got into a robe and stepped into the water. You could tell he was nervous and didn't know what to expect. He was baptized in Jesus' name for the remission of his sins. Hallelujah! But, God wasn't done with him yet. No! As soon as he came up out of the water, there were people all around praying for him, and for a mighty touch from God. The gentleman that baptized him laid one hand on my brother's head and raised the other hand to the sky, and started praying that the Lord fill him with the Holy Ghost. After a couple of seconds, my brother started speaking in tongues and started jumping up and down with much joy in his heart. He did not have a care in the world. He walked in with anguish in his heart but left with mercy and grace! He no longer felt pain, sorrow, anger, or bitterness but felt love, forgiveness, joy, and peace! I have never seen his eyes reflect such happiness. I remember the day that I received the gift of the Holy Ghost with evidence of speaking in tongues, so I know exactly what he was feeling and how happy God made him that evening! That was an amazing day that I will never forget.

I was very thankful for Serra that day. She helped me through my walk with Christ in the beginning and now had been a piece of the puzzle in my brother's beginning walk. She was the perfect person to go through this with me and to be what my brother needed to allow him to Rise and give it all to God that day. I love you, Serra! I am so very grateful for your friendship. More importantly, I appreciate your humility and your heart. Never change unless you're changing for the

Lord. Keep moving forward in the things of God, and He will always prepare the way!

God sparked a fire within our spirits that we never wanted to let burn out. Still to this day I get goosebumps just thinking about it. Obey what God asks of you, which is why I am writing this book. If I would have given up on my brother, and never went to ask him to come to church with me, even though I thought he would refuse. He would not have been saved, baptized, or filled with the Holy Ghost. If Serra wouldn't have been obedient to the Spirit and went and prayed with him then walked with him to the altar, then this part of my life might not have room in this book. The miracle in it all is that normally it is a process for most of us, but he received all three in one night. That was a miracle from God!

I share this story with you because you might be thinking of giving up on your family members. Don't! You never know what God is about to do or who He will help through you. Stay determined and be consistent because you never know when the day will come when they will say yes! God presses us, but He never pressures us! Pray for understanding about what God wants to do in your life. For now, is the time to speak up and spread the Gospel of Jesus Christ in the way that God has chosen. Everyone has a different way of expressing themselves and using their unique gifts. Find what works for you and not what works for someone else. We are in a time of spiritual warfare, so stay grounded in Jesus and be ready for battle! It is time to give that nasty ole devil an eviction notice, Amen! No matter what you face, always remember that God is still a good God even on a not-so-good kind of day!

Ye are of God, little children, and have overcome them:
because greater is he that is in you,
than he that is in the world.
I John 4:4 KJV

Start revealing who God is through you. Proclaim His Gospel through your servanthood in ministry and by sowing into the Kingdom. Step up to contributing in the lives of others more than your own. Stop on the side of the road when you see a mother and child walking with groceries because the mother has no vehicle. Start going to local jails and speak to those incarcerated. Tell them about Jesus and how He loves them even through our wrongful actions and bad decisions, and that He wants them to be better. All sins are the same in God's eyes; no matter if you kill, steal, or lie, it is all the same! Who are we to judge the sin of a man and choose who receives mercy and who doesn't? Choose to love people no matter the situation because you were once where they were. So often we forget!

Start paying for the elderly gentleman's meal that you always see eating at the same table alone at the restaurant where you eat in the mornings. We need to do more of these kinds of things. I remember a time when I stopped on the side of the highway just to give someone some water. I knew it was God, and I believe in my heart that He was testing me. God does that. He will see if you have changed or if you are still that same person that just looks at others and considers helping them, the chooses not to. This man would always ride his bike at the same time I was traveling the road. It was odd, really. I never stopped before because it seemed like I was always in a hurry to get to my destination and I never had extra water with me, nor did I stop to get some for him. But this time I stopped! This time I remembered to bring a bottle of water! This time God could use me because I made myself available!

I parked the car on the side of the highway; I ran to the gentleman that was carrying about eight bags on his bicycle that he could barely push, and I asked him if he could use some water or food. I couldn't give him a ride because I didn't have a big enough vehicle at the time, but I will never forget the look in his eyes after I asked him that question. He looked at me with so much love; I swear they seemed like they could have been the eyes of Christ. He took the water bottle, thanked me, and went on his way. Never again did I pass him on my trips down the highway. That was the last time I saw him, and I will always remember the color and beauty in those eyes. They made an image in my heart that I will never forget. That's how God thinks of you. You hold a special image in His heart, and He will never let you go.

My children know of that time and all the other things that I do in front of them just to show them that ministry is not just in the church, but is also in the streets. We need to go to people and stop waiting on people to come to us. I know it is hard to trust people, especially on the streets, but you should not be fearful.

Why do we serve God but are not willing to die for Him? I understand that we do not need to put children in danger by helping a stranger so proceed with caution, but this is something that we all need to think about. How much more could you do? How much more would you do knowing the impact you would have not only on their lives but what God would give you in return? There are times when I need to stop and don't. There are times when you know someone is hurting or needing shelter, and you don't do anything to help them out. We need to be better Christians for Jesus' sake. Are we serving Him with honor or disgrace? Good question!

Let's show people the right way to be and not act like the people of this world. Let's start doing more! Rise to the Mission, people of God. Allow others to see Jesus through you, through your actions and not just your words. Treat others how Jesus treated them when He came down from heaven to die so that we could live!

Surely goodness and mercy shall follow me all the days of my life: and I will dwell in the house of the LORD for ever.
PSALM 23:6 KJV

Be of good support to your fellow brothers and sisters in Christ. Encourage them along the way for they are on the same mission. We need to walk together side by side, not with one above, and not with one below, but just as we walk with Jesus, Amen! We need to keep telling ourselves that the things of this world are not for us. God is good, and He is faithful. We choose to serve the Lord. Why? Because He died for us so that we may be set free from our sins and have a chance to live eternally, so that we could have a relationship with God, and have the opportunity and the honor to serve Him for the purpose that only He knows.

Our mission is to successfully follow through with His vision for our lives. His Mission, Your Mission, Our Mission! What I love about this is that we all have different testimonies and different stories to tell, but we all have the same power force helping us: the power of God! When we are broken, He puts us back together stronger than our original selves. We come back wiser, tougher, more dependable, valuable, and can help others who we could not have helped before. This is the mission field for The Dreamer's Dream! The first dreamer, God Himself!

When we hep others, it brings more testimonies, salvation, healing, deliverance, and more hearts that will lay down their lives for Jesus Christ. He died for us because He truly loves us and wants to see God's will be done on earth just like it will be done in heaven. Until the day that we take our last breath, we are to serve God Almighty. After our bodies lay down, our souls will then be taken to heaven.

And this is the will of him that sent me, that every one which seeth the Son, and believeth on him, may have everlasting life: and I will raise him up at the last day.
JOHN 6:40 KJV

Walk with a humble heart, love like you are loved, seek answers to life's most important questions, and know you are worthy and cared for by your Heavenly Father. You are different than the rest, and you have been sent on a mission by God. Do not leave with unfinished business! Honor and serve each day knowing that God steps before you, beside you, and with you in every situation. We are children of the living God. We have purpose, we are unique, we are fearfully and wonderfully made in His image! Stand up, brothers and sisters, and open those arms to allow God to use you. Allow the roots of His promises to rise to where Jesus is and wrap tightly around Him so that He will always be with you.

Have not I commanded thee? Be strong and of a good courage; be not afraid, neither be thou dismayed: for the LORD thy God is with thee whithersoever thou goest.
JOSHUA 1:9 KJV

Step into the Gospel of Jesus Christ with love and a pure heart. Paul was chained in prison because he chose to preach the Gospel, but he stood firm on the promises of God. He shared the Gospel because he loved the people and was obedient unto God. When you love people, you want to help bring salvation to their lives. You want to allow God's love to show in your life and the lives of others. Sharing the Gospel of Jesus Christ is going to bring on doubt, ridicule, anger, and jealousy from some people but it will also reach the hearts of those that have ears to hear and eyes that are open and receptive.

For this reason I endure all things for the sake of those who are chosen, so that they also may obtain the salvation which is in Christ Jesus and with it eternal glory.
II TIMOTHY 2:10 NASB

Reflect on your actions and your words. Remember, love as Jesus loves. Salvation is the number one formation, and without salvation, there is no weapon of defense. With salvation, you have Jesus, and with Jesus comes power! With His power comes change, and with change comes love. With love comes mercy, and with mercy comes restoration, Glory to God! This world and the love of the world is ever-changing, but God's love never changes. We all matter no matter what we have done in our pasts or what we will do in our futures. It says in the Word of God,

And such were some of you: but ye are washed, but ye are sanctified, but ye are justified in the name of the Lord Jesus, and by the Spirit of our God.
I CORINTHIANS 6:11 KJV

Despite our pasts and who we used to be or currently are, He chooses to love us, have mercy on us, and forgive us if we give our lives to Him and ask for forgiveness.

For all have sinned, and come short of the glory of God;
ROMANS 3:23 KJV

Jesus will speak to you through the Holy Spirit as you read His Word. Every page you turn is a new beginning, a new journey, and a new relationship like you have never had before. Jesus will lift your spirits and open your heart to more understanding than you could ever imagine.

> *Jesus saith unto him, I am the way, the truth, and the life:*
> *no man cometh unto the Father, but by me.*
> JOHN 14:6 KJV

When Jesus shines through you; His love lights up the world. Be that light.

> *Ye are the light of the world. A city that is set on an hill*
> *cannot be hid. Neither do men light a candle, and put it*
> *under a bushel, but on a candlestick; and it giveth light*
> *unto all that are in the house. Let your light so shine before*
> *men, that they may see your good works, and glorify your*
> *Father which is in heaven.*
> MATTHEW 51:14-16 KJV

Seeing God's light shine in you gives others a sense of hope and freedom, knowing that His love is still burning within us, for us, and through us in Jesus Name.

The hands that lead and the steps that follow the voice of tomorrow are near. Beauty and love are carried in the calmness of the waves. They flows like the ocean waters through our veins; watch our cup overflow with the goodness thereof. He is our foundation to mold us, repair us, and fix us in abundance. When we think of Him, we think of ourselves and where we should be, only to find out where we are supposed to be through Him. He is our compass that leads us out of the darkest of storms. He is our anchor that bears deep into the barrier floors. Hope is a caption: a glimpse of what is to come. We look in the mirror and see His face; His light shines through us and His image shows from us. We hear His voice deep in our souls without fear. Just like a child holding a mother's hand tightly, the grip is unbreakable. Jesus is our brother, our

Savior, our Lord. We are joint heirs with Christ and He unfolds our purpose, guiding us along the way so that we may never again get lost or go astray. God hears our voices when we call His name because we are His children, His blood, His vision of imagination. He is our suture; our healer for the past, present, and future!

God is always faithful. No matter what we have to endure, God will always love us, and He will always be faithful to His promises.

Here is a trustworthy saying: If we died with him, we will also live with him; if we endure, we will also reign with him. If we disown him, he will also disown us; if we are faithless, he remains faithful, for he cannot disown himself.
II TIMOTHY 11:13 NIV

Get up souls, RISE TO THE MISSION! Break free from that cocoon that you have been comfortable in and get ready to grow your angel wings and fly. Learn how to be uncomfortable but get the job done; the job that God has called you to do, whatever that may be. Use those beautiful wings for His Glory!

Start loving again - yourself and others. Don't be afraid to shout it out loud that you love God and your proud! Make discoveries within yourself and the gifts of others, and start proclaiming the good news the Jesus kind of way: with LOVE and a HUMBLE heart. Shine in unity one with another, and with restoration in mind! God needs us to be bold, to be shaken up, and poured out among the world. It is time to Rise to the Mission and bring Jesus' heart back into this world. We are all called to Rise for something, so what is your reason? God gave me you and God sent you to me, so I ask Jesus to let it be! Let thy will be done on earth as it is in heaven.

It is more than just rising for one thing or the other; it is rising in all areas of your life. Take my hand and walk in faith; for I have shown you that His works are possible. Take His Word and walk with love, for the way to a man's spiritual heart is through the words and actions of the believer who testifies. Take His power and Rise above all things that may come your way; for now is the time to take your mantle and help change the world one soul at a time. Remember, many are called, but few are chosen! (Matthew 22:14). Time and eternity go hand in hand, but we treat them as insignificant gifts. Brothers and sisters, they are blessings from above, and possibilities that await us. Choose to use your time wisely so that your eternity will be filled with everlasting joy and consecrated peace. The clock is ticking…

Believe it, Receive it, and Step into your destiny, in Jesus Name.

May Our Homes Be Next to One Another in Heaven

Dear Heavenly Father, I pray that happiness comes upon this soul and that the spirit of fear is casted out of his or her mind. Father God, I ask that this individual allows you to lead his or her footsteps along their walk with you, and to stop trying to lead their own. I pray that they live their lives by faith and not by sight. I ask God that you give this soul the encouragement needed to finish the mission that you have called them to do. Father, I ask that you give them a humble heart to love others more than they love themselves. I pray that you bless their life in abundance when it comes to favor, finances, careers, friendships, and whatever they may need to succeed their journey. I pray that the person reading this today will bring in tomorrow with you in their heart, and with a new way of thinking. I pray that they always put you first and remind others that it was always because of you and not because of them, that their lives have changed and will change forevermore.

Prepare us Heavenly Father for what is to come. We are not worthy of any of it, but you still say that we are chosen to rise to the mission and be a voice of tomorrow. Allow us to love like never before, and help us lift the spirits of those who are lost but want to be found. I ask you to step before us and prepare the way; for we can do nothing without you. You are our light and shield. You protect us from our enemies and cause us to rise even when others want us to fall. We honor you Lord, and will always come after you, never before you. We give you all the glory, honor, and praise in Jesus Name, Amen!

Remember ye not the former things, neither consider the things of old. Behold, I will do a new thing; now it shall spring forth; shall ye not know it? I will even make a way in the wilderness, and rivers in the desert.

Isaiah 43:18-19 KJV

Be blessed and be a blessing to others,
~Amber~

Note from the Publisher

Are you a first time author?

Not sure how to proceed to get your book published?
Want to keep all your rights and all your royalties?
Want it to look as good as a Top 10 publisher?
Need help with editing, layout, cover design?
Want it out there selling in 90 days or less?

Visit our website for some exciting new options!

www.ingramcontent.com/pod-product-compliance
Lightning Source LLC
Chambersburg PA
CBHW071555040426
42452CB00008B/1177